Roger Canon has lived an amazing life. Like us all, he has some regrets but there are more positives to take from his experiences. To fight through dangerous situations, then only to hit rock bottom and then to climb up through to the summit of life has been an amazing journey.

Thank you to my family and friends for sticking with me when most needed.

Roger Canon

ROGER THE BOXER

I AM JUST PASSING THROUGH

AUSTIN MACAULEY PUBLISHERS™
LONDON * CAMBRIDGE * NEW YORK * SHARJAH

A CIP catalogue record for this title is available from the British Library.

ISBN 9781398435612 (Paperback)
ISBN 9781398435629 (Hardback)
ISBN 9781398435643 (ePub e-book)
ISBN 9781398435636 (Audiobook)

www.austinmacauley.com

First Published 2022
Austin Macauley Publishers Ltd®
1 Canada Square
Canary Wharf
London
E14 5AA

I would like to acknowledge the fine work of my first copy-editor, Lindsey Alexander, from Readinglisteditorial.com, and a big thank you to Austin Macauley Publishers.

Foreword

It was whilst being housebound and self-isolated due to the coronavirus, aka COVID-19, pandemic on 18 March 2020 that I started to write this book. It seemed like a good thing to do, when you are stuck in the house with lots of time on your hands. This virus started in China before Christmas and is now spreading throughout the world and taking many lives. The UK went into lockdown on 23 March indefinitely. It has been a very difficult time, and another challenge to our normal way of life. I have every confidence that our human resilience and resolve will pull us through this, and we will go on to much happier times once again.

To write a book about your life, you must adopt the 'helicopter view' and come out of yourself, then look down on the big picture. Assessing what went before this present time, with scrutiny and honesty. I have to admit, I found it much harder than I thought it would be. I have nothing but respect for those authors who can produce books on a monthly basis. I hope this book appeals to a wide spectrum of people from all walks of life. I do not like how, quite often, we tend to categorise people into certain levels of a class system. The land we live on was here long before people were, and we must respect and look after it. People came along, and civilisation began, and as it grew over the thousands of years, we developed into a have and have-not type of class system.

I have found as I have gone through my life that whoever I have come across has always got equal treatment from me. I cannot differentiate due to what that person may or may not have. We may all be very different types of people, but if you ask any older person, "What's the one thing you learnt during your life?" I bet the majority would answer, "That all people are equal to me." The Queen goes to the toilet in the same way as the rest of us do; so does the president of the USA or Russia, and all the world leaders. Famous people and very wealthy people all do the same; illnesses and accidents blight the whole human race – they do not care who you are.

Hopefully this foreword will help you to understand the type of person I am – a very down-to-earth, ordinary run-of-the-mill bloke, or, as my sons once told me, "Dad, you are the champion of everyday life." I felt honoured and blessed by that. Thank you for taking the time to read this, and I hope you enjoy reading about the ups and downs I have experienced whilst 'just passing through'.

I have not used real names, and only refer to my parents as Father or Dad and Mother or Mum. For everyone else, I have used false names or no name at all to protect their privacy. I have named a couple of well-known people and boxers, as it's impossible not to name them, but I have done so just as they are stated in the history books and records, and in a complimentary way.

Chapter One
Early Life

I was born in 1960 in North London N19, equal distance from Archway tube station and the tomb of Karl Marx in Highgate Cemetery, and a short walk to the A1 to Scotland, known as the Archway Road. My parents named me Roger, after a brother of my dad who died early in his short life as a child back in Ireland many years before. I was born into a large Catholic family, and my father came from northwest Ireland. My mother was from Scotland. When I was born, I had five brothers and two sisters older than me.

During the war, my mother worked in London in the ATS as a spotter. The spotters would shine large spotlights up into the night sky, to try to illuminate the enemy planes. My mother was stationed on top of a high building in Hanover Square, just off Regent Street in the West End of London. They were very brave, as they were often targeted themselves by the enemy aircraft. My father, who was five years younger than my mother, had a very different war, as he was too young, and he only came over after it was over, to find labouring work in Scotland.

My mother and father met when she went back home to Scotland at the end of the war in 1945. They got married shortly after. They had no money and lived in Scotland until 1954, and then lived in Ireland for a couple of years before settling in London in 1956. Whilst in Scotland they had children born: Dan, Ben, Peter, and two sisters, Molly and Freda. When in Ireland, my mother gave birth to another boy called Raymond, before they moved to live in North London, where they had my brother Stephen and finally me.

In London, my father worked hard in the tunnels below ground. With his Irish and my mother's Scottish tempers, they sometimes fought like cat and dog. I seemed destined to follow my father's way in life. I was not great at school, and I was a tough little fellow. When I was born, in 1960, our family lived in a small terraced house in North London. We then moved a short distance to a flat above a shop on the main road. My only real memories of my very early life were playing in the basement below this property. There were lots of old things from the Second World War there, like army overcoats and helmets. I can remember looking out of the front window at all the very busy traffic on the main road; I used to see a dwarf on a small motorbike quite often and I would wave to him. I don't think he ever noticed me. I can also remember walking with my mother whilst taking the others to school, and we would go up and over the *Suicide Bridge* that crossed the main road. It was called that because when the movie star Valentino died, several women threw themselves off the bridge to their deaths.

A couple of years later, I went to the local primary school with my brothers. At the weekends I can remember we used to go out to the park to play. It was just a short walk away. I have a very vivid memory of sitting on a roundabout in the park play area, when these big lads came over and jumped on it. I was sitting in the centre on top, holding on to the circular metal ball in the middle of the roundabout. They started to spin the roundabout very fast – you know, with their feet and then jumping onto it. They spun it so fast I let go of the ball and went through the air and straight into a tree, cutting my head open. I remember my two brothers getting a belting from my mother for not looking after me, as I was only about four years old.

I can remember walking with my sister in the dark one night and stopping at a building site in the pouring rain. This was one of the shafts that led down to the new underground train tunnel that my father was working on; it was around 1963. I have a picture in my head of looking over the edge of a barrier to see lots of lights at the bottom of the shaft. It looked very deep and about fifty feet in diameter around the top of the shaft. You could see little men at the bottom walking about. I learnt many years later my sister would be sent by my mother to go to my father's work to get some money from him on the Friday-payday-for her to get some groceries and such into the house. My sister would also be told to take me with her; maybe my mother wanted some peace and quiet for a while on her own.

The tunnel men who built the new underground tube line were very 'tough men'. Many of them were from Ireland and known as the 'Tunnel Tigers'. They used to drink in the large local pub; they called it their 'office'. They worked in compressed air for many hours and had to decompress in a special chamber after work. How long they were supposed to remain in the chamber depended on how many hours they had worked, but they would bang on the door to be let out early, when the pubs opened, and the man would let them out early. Later that night, anyone who wasn't properly decompressed would collapse in the pub and be rushed to hospital with the bends (nitrogen bubbles in their blood). This happened to my father more than once.

I remember we had a German shepherd dog that would carry me around the garden on its back. Then one day it bit me on the face and I never saw it again. I think my father gave it to someone. I had one memory of losing teeth; my mother would always say in a nice, soft voice, "Let me have a look at your loose tooth." Then she would feel it nice and gently, then *wham*! She would pull it out, and I'd have a mouth full of blood. I got wise to this, though. When I had a loose tooth and I wouldn't let her near it, no matter how soft and gentle her voice was, she grabbed me and put her fingers in my mouth and tried to yank the tooth out, but because I was wriggling about so much, it was only half pulled out and hung from a piece of my gums. I ran outside and into the outside toilet. I quite liked the outside toilet, as it was like a small place of solace for me, with its ball on the end of a chain that I couldn't quite reach, and squares of newspapers on a piece of string nailed to the wall. I managed to get the tooth pulled out, and that night I hid it under my pillow for the tooth fairy. In the morning I had a silver sixpence under my pillow.

I remember my father telling my mother a funny story about his day at work. He drove a little Austin A40 car then, and he had a problem with it starting. If he turned it off, he wasn't sure if it would start again. He had been driving through Hertfordshire past this large mental hospital when he got a puncture. He stopped and left the engine running whilst he took the wheel off to replace it with the spare from the boot of the car. As he undid each wheel nut, he placed each nut onto the wing of the car. When he got the spare wheel on and in place, he looked up and noticed that with the vibrations of the running engine all the wheel nuts had fallen from the wing and gone down the drain gulley in the road beside him. He stood up, scratching his head, when he noticed an inmate from the mental hospital sitting on the perimeter wall watching him. My father said to him, "Where is the nearest garage to here?" The inmate said, "It's about three miles that way, but you don't have to walk there. Why don't you take one of the wheel nuts off each of your three other wheels, use them to fasten the fourth wheel into place, and then you can drive to the garage with three-wheel nuts holding each wheel in place, to get it fixed properly." My father was amazed at this chap's clever thinking and said, "That's very helpful, and if you don't mind me saying, why are you in the mental hospital, as you sound very clever to me." The man replied, "They can't let me out until I get a job." My father said as a thank-you, "When I get back to the office, I'll see if my boss will give you a job and get you out of this place." My father jotted down his name and details and then started to drive off towards the garage. Then there was this almighty *smash*, and a brick came right through the back window of the car. My dad got out and looked back, and this inmate shouted, "You won't forget, will you?"

Chapter Two
The South Coast

I lived in North London until 1966. That summer we moved to the South Coast, as my father had work on a new bypass road scheme. We lived in a council house in not the best of areas that was full of people who didn't like to obey the law. I have a vivid memory of me and two of my brothers walking over to the field behind our house and road, to play football with some of the local boys who were kicking a ball about.

It didn't start very well as these kids with their leader, who was probably eleven or twelve, stood right in front of us and went through the usual ritual of 'you are the new kids around here'. This leader boy moved closer to my brother, so I whacked him in the face, and then it all went mad, but us three were used to far harsher fights in London, and we smashed the tougher ones up and the others ran away. After that we were always welcomed to play football, and the three of us were now part of the local area's tough boys. We all went through the same experience when we started school. I got in with one good lad who I am still friends with to this day – that's fifty-four years of friendship. I quite enjoyed school, but trouble always seemed to follow me through the next couple of years. I was always nicking bottles of milk or apples at school, and outside school nicking bottles of fizzy drink from lorries parked outside the factory. We had a nice lady teacher who took me and my mate for a day trip to Arundel Castle with her boyfriend on a Saturday. I don't know if they would be allowed to do that anymore with today's restrictions. We had a great time, and it was the first real castle I had ever seen. There was a park behind it with a rowing lake in it. I remember they bought us ice creams and took us out into the lake on a boat. I never knew why she did all that for us; I think she felt sorry for us – what a terrific lady.

At the bottom of our road you had the sea, not the proper sea, but water anyway that must have been an inlet from the sea. The other side of the water was a small island that was a Royal Navy base. It was an adventure park to us and a very secret place that we would see every day from our shores, but it was heavily guarded with barriers and guards on the other side of a large road bridge that went from our mainland to the island. We could walk along the bridge, and if the tide was out, we could look over the edge of the bridge and see a concrete road that was submerged underwater; it ran the whole way under the bridge and beside it to the island. If the tide was out, there would only be about two feet of water covering the road, and hundreds of flat fish, I think they were flounders or skates, would be sitting on the concrete road under the water. They looked amazing from where we were, high up on the bridge. If we turned around and went to the other side of the bridge, we could see a marina with loads of boats, mostly small to medium size, apart from one extremely big boat that was called the *Britannia*, the Queen's yacht, and it was always parked in the marina beside the island until she needed to use it. Once a year in the hot summer, we were allowed onto the island for the navy's open weekend. This was for a military show where they would do all their practising of the 'Gun Run' for the royal show at Earl's Court or Wembley later in the year. This was a great time for us, as we could explore the island as much as allowed to within the security confines.

Once we went right to the back of the island, and on the stones of the beach, there were lots of little rowing boats. We could jump in and out of them playing, and pretend to be Sir Francis Chichester, who had rowed around the world on his own. Where the main Gun Run area was there were large tents for the sailors to change and get ready. They would have several crates of large milk bottles full of milk to drink when they finished the gun run. We would sneak our hands up under the edge of the tent and nick a couple of bottles, then drink the milk out of sight.

There was this large rope hanging from an enormous tree. I think they used it to practice swinging on. When it swung, you could go from the top of one hill across to the top of the other hill. There were about five of us, and we started to swing, and then as the rope came back to one hill, another lad would jump on until all five of us were hanging from this rope, over a twenty-foot drop below us. I let go and fell, and all I remember was waking up on a fold-up bed in a navy tent with a nurse talking to me, and then they gave me a drink of milk and let me out to join up with the other lads, who were all laughing and calling me a plonker.

The actual gun runs were very exciting to watch, and they were real tough sailors, as many times one would fall under the wheels of the cannon they had built as they raced alongside the other navy team, all running to get to the end first and fire their cannon and be declared the winners. Sometimes they would be hanging on to a fast-moving wire, holding a cannon wheel with one arm and the wire with the other. They were always losing a finger or getting their arms or legs broken.

We had to go to the large Catholic church beside our junior school every Sunday with our father. I hated it and found it very boring; it just seemed to go on forever. Sometimes we could sneak out pretending we weren't feeling well. We could then get a lump of coal from the caretaker's shed and play football with it in the school playground. When we saw our father coming out at the end of mass, we'd run up behind him and pretend we had been in the church all the time but sitting in a different place.

I remember I was sent away on a short holiday in the summer for two or three days with these people from our church. I think they did it as a charity for children. I don't know the details as I was very young at the time. We stayed in a large house like a boarding school, as it had a dormitory with lots of beds in it. Whilst there, we visited an American army base, which was very exciting, and I saw this large American car, like the ones I had seen on the TV. In the canteen they gave us a drink of American root beer. I had never tasted anything like it before; it was like scented Coca-Cola. Years later McDonald's sold it. I had a good trip, even though it was with a load of complete strangers and children I had never met before.

We used to have most things delivered in the sixties, like newspapers, milk, bread, and green groceries. The man who used to deliver green groceries in our area sometimes would pop into a house for a cup of tea and a chat; that was always our chance to nick things from his cart. Sometimes he'd come running out of the house and chase us, but we always got away. One day at home in our house, I was sitting in front of the black-and-white TV on the floor when my sister came in with her new boyfriend to introduce him to our mother and father. Wouldn't you believe it, but it was the green grocery delivery man. Me and my brothers just turned our backs on him sharpish, before he could recognise us. My other sister, Molly, was married to a man called Kevin from Ireland. Kevin had worked on the tunnels for a bit with my father and was a digger driver at that time, before he became a self-employed general builder.

I enjoyed my time living on the South Coast from 1966 up to 1974. I had done a fair bit of my childhood there. I loved football and had trials with the local main professional football club. The coach was great and had us running on the stones beside the sea. I even got to play on the main pitch in the club stadium. Alas, I didn't get selected for the elite youngsters, probably because I was quite small then, but I did have broad shoulders. I settled in to playing for my school and then the secondary school.

We often went to watch the football club, who were in the old second division. We got to see an old Dave McKay (great ex-Spurs player) player/manager for Swindon Town FC, and George Best played in a pre-season friendly for Manchester United. I remember seeing them play Burnley FC in the pouring rain. Me and my mate had climbed up on to the bottom of the large concrete base of the floodlight to get a better view, and we got drenched whilst watching great Burnley players like Ralph Coates and Dave Thomas, the fast winger with his socks down around his ankles. Even at the age of ten, I was a little sod as I remember, they were playing a London team called Leyton Orient in a cup game, and after the match we were walking through a graveyard that had a large perimeter wall around it. All we could see was about two feet of the Orient fans' coaches above the wall as they slowly moved along in the traffic. We got these small rocks from a couple of graves and started to throw them at the coaches. There were about ten of us wearing scarfs. I saw one of these rocks thrown by the lad next to me smash a coach back window, and then loads of red and white scarfs were coming out of the coach and over the wall. We ran for our lives through the graveyard and down the alleyways and shortcuts we knew and they didn't. It was a lucky escape.

I remember being so cold at night times, we had old overcoats on the bed to keep us warm, with three of us boys in the same bed. I would usually be in the middle getting squashed. I remember one Christmas I couldn't get to sleep, and I rubbed the ice off the inside of the bedroom window, looking at the night sky and the stars. It must have been a shooting star as I saw this white thing flying across the sky. I thought it was Father Christmas, so I quickly jumped back into bed and shut my eyes in case he saw me looking at him. What sweet innocence. When we got up at 5:00 a.m., we each had a pillowcase with our presents in them. I remember there was always a little tangerine and a variety bag with sweets in it. My main present was an Action Man toy figure, but he only had one arm, as my mother had bought it from a jumble sale. I didn't care; he was great to me, and I made it up that he had lost his arm in battle. I used to slide him down the washing line, him holding on with his one arm; it was great fun.

My last year at junior school, in 1971/72, we were the first pupils not to take the eleven plus exam that determined if you went to secondary or grammar school. We were instead evaluated on our year's work and a small test paper. I passed and was given a place at a top grammar school. When a letter arrived from the grammar school listing everything that I would need when starting in September, my mother nearly fainted. It was all sorts of sports kits and uniforms, etc. My mother told me she could not afford any of that, and I would have to go to the comprehensive school with my two older brothers and wear their old uniforms that were now too small for them, along with scuffed-up shoes. They got new uniforms that were far too big. That was how they did things then, with a 'you'll grow into it soon enough' statement that made it all okay then. I was sad not to go to the better school, as we used to go past it every day sitting upstairs on the bus, and you could see all their cricket nets and the rugby and hockey pitches. I consoled myself that I would have been one of only two to go there from my junior school, and all my school friends were going to the comprehensive as well.

The first year in any secondary school is going to be tough, especially at the start, but I was lucky to have my two older brothers already in the school; that gave me a certain amount of protection from the bullies. I was also a tough kid, having been fighting all my life. I could take a good punch, and often my mother would be called to the school and questioned by the teachers. They wanted to know why when they hit me, I just laughed at them. The more they hit me, the more I laughed. My mother had to explain to them it was nervous energy, and it was how I handled pain or violence. She told them I was exactly the same when at home.

This trick of mine would come in handy later in my life when I became an amateur boxer. I knew how to handle pain. I became the best fighter in the first year at school, and I had a couple of good friends around me as well. I liked the swimming pool in the school. Why don't schools seem to care much about swimming anymore? Most of the modern schools nowadays have no swimming pools and limited access to leisure centres as well. I did the bronze survival badge, where you had to swim a length in your pyjamas, then tread water whilst taking the bottoms off, tie the legs in knot, then swing them over your head to fill them with air, then use them as a temporary float. You also had to dive down to the deep end (about 1.8m deep) and pick up a rubber brick and swim underwater with it for a certain length of metres. I really enjoyed getting the bronze badge to go on my swimming trunks. I never got the silver or gold, as we moved back to London before I could get them.

I remember one of the boys in our class at school had an electric guitar, as his older brothers were also guitarists and in their own band. I went back to his house with him a couple of times. He would plug his guitar into a massive sound speaker, and he would play the chords and the intro of the song, *Radar Love* by the band Golden Earring. It was fantastic, and I remember looking in this music shop near my school at all the guitars and drum kits. I would have loved to play an instrument, especially drums, but we had no money and I don't think the neighbours would have been too pleased if I had a drum kit. It seemed my destiny was to be a fighter and not a musician.

Stephen and I were mostly just playing football all the time. I remember Stephen being a very good left back in the school football team. They had a very good team, and they got to the county cup semi-final, where they came up against a team who were brilliant. The match was at a semi-professional team's ground that had a distinct slope to it. My brother's team started the first half going down the slope, and they were 3–0 up at half-time. Stephen had to mark their best player, who happened to play for England schoolboys. He was very tall and slim and as sharp as a razor. The other team won the match 3–5, and the player Stephen was marking scored three goals. Stephen said afterwards that he couldn't even get close enough to him to foul him. That lad went on to play for Chelsea and QPR. My football for our school team wasn't very exciting, and we just plodded along in mid-table.

We moved from our house a couple of miles north to a nicer house. I liked it there, although it was farther to go to school. It was quite a short road on a gradient going up towards a large hill and the white chalk cliffs above. Me and my mates would go around the houses washing cars for a few shillings here and there. My father used to use a couple of pubs in the centre of the town. These pubs were managed by a big Irish man with a big beer belly. My father was good friends with him, and they would often drink long after closing. One time my mother told me to go to the pub to see if I could get him to come home for the Sunday dinner. He told me to wait outside and he'd be out soon. I sat outside for what seemed like ages. There was a lot of noise and shouting coming from inside the pub, then the door burst open and my father and the guvnor of the pub came flying out throwing punches at each other. They went out into the road and onto the pavement on the other side still punching each other, until a black police van arrived and loads of coppers threw them both in the back and drove away.

I thought it was hysterical and I couldn't wait to tell my mother when I got home. The next day my father had a big shiner of a black eye, and he was back in the pub drinking with the guvnor again, all hostilities forgotten over a pint.

When I was told I would be returning to London when school finished in July 1974, I was very upset, and I really did not want to go. I had made good friends and was respected as a tough kid, with a few girls chasing me as well. On my last day at school, three or four girls made me go to a passport photo booth with them, to have our photos taken together.

Chapter Three
Return to London

We returned to London to a council house in the northwest part of the city, less than a mile from the old Wembley Stadium with the iconic twin towers. I was far from happy but had no choice but to accept it. The first thing I noticed were the people of all different colours and races, very different to where I had been living in the years before 1974. The house was semi-detached, at the end of a cul-de-sac. It was the last house in the road with a fence separating us from a river and a recreational field. The other side of the park was some houses and an old railway line, then the back of Wembley Stadium.

I remember standing in our garden and listening to the noises from the old stadium, like the world speedway finals, England football matches, and of course pop concerts with Rod Stewart, Elton John, and other various acts of the time. The lights would light up the sky above the stadium, like a fire going from earth to sky. In the garden there was a large disused pigeon shed against the wall. It had small square windows with no glass, only slats of wood. I removed alternate slats from the windows to create a mix of holes into the shed. I could then kick my football into the different holes to score a goal. I would pretend I was the centre forward for my beloved team, Spurs, playing against Arsenal with a running commentary in my head. Spurs always won, of course, and it was great shooting practice for me.

I had about a six-week holiday before starting school. Some days I would wander up to Wembley Stadium, and the large doors to the tunnel were often open. I could walk in and up the famous tunnel. I would sit on one of the old wooden benches at ground level by the terraces, maybe thirty feet from the pitch. I could watch the groundsmen working on the pitch. The white goalposts would be lying on the grass at the side of the pitch. If a groundsman walked past me, he would just say, "How are you, son," and walk on, smiling. What fantastic innocent times, and great memories for a young schoolboy to keep forever. Nowadays you wouldn't get anywhere near the place. I also used to go out on my own to catch a train from the nearest train station; it was just a short walk along the main road. I would get off the train after a few stops at Queens Park Station, where you could get on to an underground tube train into London on the Bakerloo line. I spent a couple of days a week doing this and just getting off at any stop I felt like. I got lost many times, but I always seemed to find my way back home okay. When I think back now, I must have been a very confident thirteen-year-old to mix with all those London people and not know where I was.

After a couple of weeks my sister and her husband took me and my brother back to their house in the home counties, to stay with them for a couple of weeks to help Kevin on his building sites. This was very tough work. Kevin had been doing an extension on a big house. He would get us up at 6:00 a.m., and we would walk about a mile to get a green line country bus to the site. We wouldn't get home until after 6:00 p.m. I was only thirteen years old, and it was a very tough time for me and Stephen, who was fifteen at the time. He worked us hard and paid me £2 a day and Stephen £5 for labouring. That included digging drain runs to soakaways, and foundations for the extension to the house.

I remember one day we had to repoint the chimney stack. Kevin only had a long three-piece ladder going up to just about one foot past the roof gutters. He then climbed up the roof slates to the chimney, with me behind him with a bucket of mortar and the pointing trowel in it. I felt like I was going to slide down the slates and off the edge. It was a good three floors up to the top of this large house. Kevin was whistling away pointing, with me flat on the roof holding the bucket. This large black cloud had come over us and there was a loud crack, then the rain came pelting down. I started to slide on the shiny slates and grabbed Kevin's leg, then I slid slowly down the tiles and managed to get my foot onto the top of the ladder. I had to let go of the bucket and that had gone crashing to the ground, where it broke into many pieces. Kevin slid down from above me, and we manged to get down to the ground, soaking wet but still in one piece. I wonder what the HSE would make of that nowadays, and me just thirteen years old. I worked for Kevin quite a lot on different sites, either digging, laying drains, or labouring on him to lay bricks. I learnt loads from him, and it would help to shape me as a man years later.

We were on a site in North London laying a long run of drainage pipes through the back garden of this building. We had to fit a pipe stopper into one end of the drain run and fill the run of pipes up with water. We were supposed to leave them overnight, and in the morning you would see if the water had lowered, telling you there was a leak in the pipe joints, before the building inspector arrived to inspect the pipes and pass them or fail them. There was also a trick of breaking a matchstick in half and putting it onto the water at the top of the pipe bend. If the matchstick spun around, you had a leak somewhere. Kevin was telling me how years ago they could trick the inspector by placing a balloon just past the downward bend of the top pipe, meaning there were only a few inches of water in the entire run of pipes, as the balloon was stopping any water getting past it, then you could just pop the balloon once the inspector had gone.

I thought I would be clever and ran over the road to a shop, where I bought a packet of balloons. When I returned, unknown to me, the building inspector had arrived and was now talking to Kevin. I walked up to them and said, "Here's those balloons you wanted, Kev." Kevin went bright red and snatched them from me, saying, "Oh yes, those are for my daughter's party tonight." The building inspector to his credit just laughed and said nothing, and he passed the pipes anyway. There was no need for balloons, as Kevin was a very good builder who knew what he was doing.

On the next job we were underpinning a bungalow in Hertfordshire. Underpinning involved putting in new foundations under the existing foundations of a house. You would dig down about 600mm below the existing foundation in a hole one metre by one metre square. Then miss a metre and dig another one-metre hole. This was continued all the way around the perimeter of the house. Once you had concreted and dry-packed the one-metre sections, it could be backfilled. Then you could start again, digging out the one-metre sections not already dug out. When you finished, there was a complete perimeter of new foundation underneath the existing foundation, which was defective or cracked. The underpinning was tough. It would take the skin off your knuckles and hurt your back, and many times you were standing in six inches of water. Then of course you had to get the earth out into a skip on the road.

The harsh work is what is called 'character building'. I had no complaints and I enjoyed it all. I have recalled those harsh feelings many times as I have gone through many difficult experiences since then, and it has helped me massively to overcome hard times, so thank you, Kevin, for being such an inspiration to me, and toughening me up.

We had a big school a ten-minute walk away from our house. Unfortunately, one of the teachers there had been stabbed, so my mother said no way and took us to a school a few miles away on the bus. It was still a rough school with no uniform. I got to go to school each day in jeans and Doc Marten boots and a T-shirt and Harrington jacket – it was great. I was still unhappy being in this strange city of London, after moving back from the South Coast, but as the summer went on, I started to accept the situation. My first day at school arrived, and I was placed in the top class of the third year, 3A. We had a gorgeous blond teacher, who always wore nice skirts just above her knees and stockings. All the boys were in love with her, me included. We would drop pens on the floor so we could have a peek up her skirt; we thought she knew, as she would often have her legs open a few inches. This meant we could see her stocking tops and knickers.

I sat next to a lad who was also from a big Irish family. At the first break time, I went out to the playground. I was amazed at all the black faces; that I was just not used to. The tough kids came up to me, led by this big lad of about six feet tall. They asked me all about myself and took the mickey out of my accent, but I think they realised I wasn't scared of them, so they accepted me as part of the group. We went on to become great friends, and we all kept in touch for many years after leaving school. The biggest fights I had in those early days happened when I was getting on the bus. It was always packed. I hated it, and I used to walk most of the time, with just the occasional jump onto the open back platform of the bus. I'd go a bit, until the conductor came down the stairs, then I'd jump off.

I did okay at school without breaking any records, and I was an average pupil. A few times we would meet in the local café before school, go to school for the registration, then jump over the fence and meet back in the café. Then we would get a red bus rover ticket for the buses. This could be used on any bus in the whole of London. We'd go to the museums in South Kensington, where we could take the mickey out of other kids our age, who were on a school trip to the museums with their teachers. Then we'd meet other kids who were also bunking off school and we could fight them. Some of them came from Brixton in South London, or even Bethnal Green in East London. They came from all over London.

After a couple of months, I was settling in nicely. One of my older brothers had bought a house on the South Coast near to where we used to live. He worked abroad, and his wife stayed at home. I received a letter from my best pal from there, telling me this kid who was accepted as the second-best fighter in my year at school behind me had been bullying a couple of my old friends who had not mixed with this kid. Our school half-term holidays differed between there and London, so I got a train down and stayed with my sister-in-law for a couple of days. The word had spread through the school third year, that I was coming back from London to beat this bully up.

I turned up at the school gates as they were all coming out to go home. My former friends greeted me, then this bully came out and walked straight up to me and said something not very nice. I hit him with a couple of quick punches, knocking him to the floor. He stumbled to get up from the ground and started to run away, but I ran alongside him and hit him with a great right-hand punch, knocking him out on to the ground. I then kicked him a few times. My friends pulled me off and away from him. I got back to my sister-in-law's house a bit later that evening with scratched knuckles, and there was a police officer there waiting to talk to me. This kid was in hospital with suspected brain damage; he went on to make a full recovery. I think they just wanted it to sound much worse than what it was. The police officer told me to go in the garden whilst he spoke in private with my sister-in-law. I can remember him saying, "Can he escape from the garden?" which I thought was a strange thing to say. I was called back in and given the ultimatum. The police officer was taking me directly to the train station and escorting me onto the next train to London. I was to tell my parents what had happened, because they would be getting a letter in the post in the next couple of days, saying I was charged with violent behaviour and I would receive a police caution.

That train journey was my longest journey ever. The whole way I was thinking how I was going to tell my parents. I knew my mother would be upset and would tell my father, who could react in several ways. The worst being giving me a good hiding. I got home and went straight to bed. I did not tell them and waited for the letter to arrive. The letter arrived on my first day back at school. I got home from school and my mother went mad at me, but she didn't hit me, which was a surprise. She said she would leave that to my father. I didn't see my father until the next day. He had been drinking, and I could smell the usual whiskey smell coming from him. He shouted at me and grabbed me by the throat, lifting me up and pinning me to the wall. He was most upset that I had kicked the kid on the floor. In his old ways, you were supposed to let the man get up, then knock him back down again to prove you were the better man. He thought kicking a man on the ground was cowardly. What he didn't realise was I was now being brought up in London, and in a very dangerous area. I had learnt that a man, or in my case another boy, could get up off the floor and stab you and kill you.

My father did not hit me. I do not know why. Maybe he felt I was a chip off the old block and too much like him. In my father's mind, you had to either be a drinker or a fighter to be a real man. I turned out to be a fighter, then a drinker when I got into my thirties. The day arrived when my father and I had to attend the local police station, to go before a chief inspector, who would give me the official caution for my violent behaviour. It wasn't as bad as I thought it would be. The officer spoke calmly but with authority, and he made it clear to me, "There were two paths in life, and being in front of him was the wrong one." I was told to wait outside whilst the officer spoke with my father in private. We left the police station and walked home. My father was very quiet, and I could imagine he was still upset from what the officer had said to him, probably something along the lines of he was not being a very good parent. Knowing my father, he was probably very close to hitting the police officer, as he never had much time for them, or for authority in general.

Back at school I was the bee's knees as everyone heard about me going to the police station. Some of my friends at school had been done for minor things. I won a couple of fights at school to cement my place amongst the tough lads. I fought one big West Indian kid who was in the year below me, and I smashed him up, but the problem was he had an older brother in the same year as my older brother. Word went around this older brother was looking for me to smash me up. This older brother of the kid I beat up caught up with me after school. I was in the fourth year at school, and he was in the sixth year, but I battered him. It wasn't easy and I took a few good shots, but like most of my fights, I could take a punch and it didn't bother me to get hit, as I was in it for the long term and I would keep laughing at my opponent, who would then realise he had made a big mistake. Next day at school I had a bruise under my eye, but everyone congratulated me on winning the fight, except the headmaster, that is. I got the cane yet again.

The next time I visited the South Coast from London was with my parents and two brothers to visit my sister Freda. My father parked the car outside someone's house near my sister's house, but it had a small sign on the garden fence saying, *do not park here – In use 24 hours*. My father said it was a public road with no dropped-down kerb, and the homeowner couldn't tell people not to park there.

When we came back to the car to drive back to London, the man in the house came out and started shouting at my father: "I'm an ex police officer and I need that space kept clear." Not a good thing to say. My father hit him, and they both wrestled and fell through the fence, flattening all the flower beds. We were sitting in the car with my mother watching this and cheering him on. The woman in the house came running out screaming, "My flowers! My flowers!" with her husband getting a beating on his back. This even made my mother laugh. We drove back to London with my father swearing most of the way and driving like a lunatic.

One thing I had noticed about London being very different from the South Coast was the standard of football. I was one of the best players at my previous school, and yet now I couldn't even get in the team – I was a reserve. The team was excellent and went unbeaten in all competitions for two seasons, and to do that was amazing. Every game was a win: 13–0, 12–1, or 16–2, and so on. We had several lads who represented the county (Middlesex) and were on the books of top professional teams. I eventually got into the team, and I enjoyed playing left midfield or forward on the left wing. I also played for a Sunday league team affiliated with the local Catholic church. We were in two Sunday leagues, the morning and the afternoon leagues. We'd play in the morning, then go home and have dinner before meeting up again to play the second match in the afternoon. We were pretty good, and we were the same team in both leagues, but not as good as the best team in the morning, who wore an all-green strip, and they were then called a different name in the afternoon league wearing a yellow strip.

They were the same team, with just one or two different players for the afternoon. They had about eight of our school team in their side. In our team there were only two of us from our school team, but we did have a good kid at left back, who went on to play for Nottingham Forest and England years later. We came runners up in both Sunday leagues and lost in both Cup finals. On one Sunday our manager said, "Next Sunday we haven't got any matches, as you lot will be ball boys at Wembley Stadium for the FA Vase Trophy Cup final between Epsom and Ewell and Hoddesdon Town and a celebrity charity match before it." It was April 1975, and we were very excited. We arrived and had to change in the men's toilets in the famous tunnel. Of course, I knew the tunnel very well, from all the times I had been in it during the summers.

We lined up in the tunnel alongside the celebrities. I cannot remember them all, but there was Gareth Edwards and Barry John from rugby union, DJ Ed 'Stewpot' Stewart, pop group Dave Dee, Dozy, Beaky, Mick, and Tich. There were rumours beforehand that Rod Stewart and Elton John would be playing, but that turned out to be a wind-up.

We led the teams out from the tunnel and across the pitch from behind the goal, just like you see on FA Cup Final day on the TV. I thought the grass was like carpet and your boots sank into it. It was a great experience. I think Hoddesdon won the trophy, which was the first-ever FA Vase Cup Final.

Whilst at school in the seventies, just about every boy had a Saturday job. Apart from working on the building sites with Kevin in the summer, my first job was in a local greengrocer shop in a small parade of shops, just a ten-minute walk from my house. Unfortunately, the first job the owner gave me was to sit out the back of the shop and sort out the crates of lovely cherries. I had to put all the good ones into one crate and throw all the bad ones with marks on them into another crate. We never had cherries in our house ever, so you can imagine what was coming. After ten minutes the boss came out to check on me, and there weren't many good cherries in the crate, but quite a few bad ones in the other crate, and me sitting there with bright red lips. My new job lasted all of thirty minutes. I walked home laughing and eating the cherries that were in my pocket.

Then I got a job with a friend, who was already working in a good butcher shop. It was opposite a bus garage in the busy high street. It was hard work from 7:00 a.m. to 6:00 p.m. for £6. The shop was the busiest butcher shop in the whole of the borough; a queue would start at about 8:00 a.m. and still be out of the door until past 5:00 p.m. It was nonstop all day. There were five butchers in the shop, including the boss, and one senior butcher out the back along with us two Saturday boys. Our job out the back was to clean out the innards from the chickens the customers had bought, put the giblets into a small bag, and put that back into the chicken, before wrapping it up and taking it back up to the shop, shouting the person's name and handing it over to them.

Sometimes I would go out on deliveries to places not too far away, like the bakers over the road, or a lady who was disabled and lived a few roads behind the shop. I used to deliver pork mince to a Chinese restaurant halfway up the high road. They would always complain the mince had too much fat in it, and I'd have to take it back, then return with the mince being more lean this time.

Although the restaurant was fronted by a Chinese family, it was rumoured to be owned by Roger Moore and Peter Sellers, the famous actors, but I never knew if that was true or not, and I still don't. It was very elitist and expensive, though, and apparently you could not book a table, as you had to be put on a waiting list first. The restaurant was just past Morgan Studios on the high road where Rod Stewart had recorded an album called *Smiler* in 1974. The hit single, *Whoa, I'm Going to Barbados* was also recorded there.

Working in the butchers was good fun, and all the older butchers told us stories from the Second World War, and they were real characters who talked 'back slang'. They would say a word but as if it was spelt backwards, like *gib* was *big*, and *Eros* was *sore*, etc. They were always playing up to the lady shoppers, and two butchers would shout to one another in the shop things like 'Gib T. Serbs', meaning 'big breasts'. They could bend the spellings to sound good and not be too easy for people to realise what they were saying. At Christmas we could do extra shifts, mainly making beef or pork sausages, or plucking turkeys, guinea fowl, and pheasants. We would have blisters on our fingers from so much plucking. I worked every Saturday there for two years, and I learnt a lot about butchery.

When I was fifteen years old, my father took me and my brother on holiday to his birthplace in Ireland. I remember he took us to the clothes shop to get a suit each, including a waistcoat. It was dark blue and not expensive, but I felt very grown up in it. It was a very long journey to Ireland. We got the train to Holyhead, which took forever, then a ferry boat over to Dublin. The boat was packed with all the Irish families from all over the UK, going home for the summer holidays. All the adults were in the bar, and it was packed and full of smoke, and the toilets were full of drunk men throwing up. We stayed outside and watched all the waves crashing against the front of the boat. It would take about four hours to get to Dublin.

We stayed the night in a small bed and breakfast, with my dad in one bed and me and my brother sharing the other. We went out for a walk along O'Connell Street to a river at the end. This old tramp was banging the shop windows trying to break one. My father said, "He is just looking to get arrested to get a bed for the night."

The next day we caught a small old bus heading north and west out of Dublin. It took all day. We then caught another bus for about an hour out to the hills and mountains and the small village where my father was from. This last small country bus stopped in the middle of nowhere and just sat there for about ten minutes. Being from the big city, I was getting impatient, and I asked my father what was going on. He said the driver is probably picking someone up, and then this old lady and her dog came over the field and got on the bus – I couldn't believe it and off we went again, trundling along these tiny country roads surrounded by hills and mountains.

My father was right when he said, "You can throw your watch away when you come here." We stayed with my father's sister (my auntie), her husband, and their children in a very old cottage, where my father's father had lived and died. I had a great time with my cousins there, and they even took us out with them to a dance in a great big marquee, which was a good hour drive away in a minibus. We had loads to drink, and it was all very noisy and crowded. I remember being in the back of the bus behind the seats by the back doors, and it was rocking all over the place. It was about 4:00 a.m. when we finally got to bed.

The next day at breakfast my auntie asked me, "Did you have a good time at the dance last night?" In my innocence, I replied, "I don't know, I was too pissed!" All my cousins just burst out laughing.

Later that day me and my cousin who was the closest age to me went out into the hills. We climbed up this massive hill and crept up and jumped, trying to catch this little rabbit, expecting it to run away. But it just sat there. We noticed its eyes were white, and my cousin said he thought it had myxomatosis and was probably blind and deaf and just waiting to die. I was a bit sad after that, but when we got back to their house, we tried riding the youngest of their two donkeys. My cousin slapped the donkey when I had just got on to it, and it ran down this steep slope with me around its neck screaming. Typical city kid.

The next day we all went out with the donkey and cart into the fields to cut and stack turf (peat), and to bring a load of it back and stack it in this big shed, to keep dry for the winter fires. We had a great time in Ireland, but I was glad to get back to the noise of London. Ireland has been in my heart ever since that first holiday in 1975, and I still go there when I can to see my wonderful cousins. I also have cousins in Scotland. My father drove us up to Scotland in 1974. The main town looked a bit like London to me, with lots of flats and tenement blocks. They were real characters, and they had it just as tough as we did in London. We did go to the Highlands of Scotland once when I was about four years old, but I have little memory of it and we never went there again.

Chapter Four
Boxing

The friend I sat with in school joined a boxing club, and he asked me to come. He said, "You'd be well suited to boxing, Rog. You're a good fighter." The club was a long way on the bus. I loved the gym the minute I walked in. There were junior boxers at one end and senior boxers at the other end, with a boxing ring in the centre. There were probably forty boxers in all. The smell and the noise of punch bags being hit, the trainers barking out instructions, the skipping ropes turning at vast speeds – it all seemed fantastic. Being a boy's club and not just a boxing club meant we could play snooker, table tennis, pool, or darts after we finished training, which was great. They also had four football teams, and in one season they won the league and cup double at all four age groups. One of their players went on to play for Watford, Liverpool, and England.

I took to boxing straight away, but I was not naturally gifted. Everything I did I had to work very hard at, but that was where I excelled, as I had always been used to hard work and I was tougher than the average kid. The trainers were Tony, who was head of all training, with Jim helping him as he had just finished boxing himself. Looking after the juniors and us new kids was Jake. He was a real character in his late sixties. Jake had been a professional boxer before and during the war. In those days, you would have hundreds of bouts just to get a few shillings to put food on the table.

Jake told me some great old boxing stories. Once he was boxing on a Sunday at Lime Grove Baths in Shepherd's Bush. It was his third fight of the day, and he had a few pounds to come at the end of the day. He was getting a bit of a beating and had a cut eye when he sat down on the stool at the end of the fifth round. A bloke stuck his head through the ropes and said to Jake, "I wouldn't try too hard, mate. The promoter has done a bunk with all the money." Jake laughed and told me, "What could I do other than cry?" There was also Sam, who helped with the training, but he was mostly the competition secretary, and his role was to arrange all the fights between other club boxers and ours for boxing shows all over London.

How it worked in amateur boxing was you had to prove you were capable of boxing and representing the club. You could then be put forward by your trainer to have an ABA (Amateur Boxing Association) full medical. Once you had passed this, the ABA would send the club an official blue record book for you. This book was used to record all the bouts you had at the various boxing shows throughout your amateur career. I got stuck into the job in hand and trained hard on Tuesday, Friday, and Sunday mornings. I loved it.

The long journey on the bus was a nuisance, especially coming home at about 10:00 p.m. There were often very unsavoury people got on the bus, many times arguing with the conductor or just in groups and messing about around me. On more than one occasion the bus would stop and wait for the police to arrive. I would have to get off and walk the rest of the way, then get up for school the next day. I had just turned fourteen years old. After a couple of months, I had my full medical, and I was ready for my first bout. It happened at a working men's club in Kilburn in June 1975. I was up against a boy from a good boxing club. It was a very tough bout that I won on points by a majority decision (two judges to one). I had a split lip and a bloody nose, but I felt fantastic and I got a nice shiny trophy as well. My trainer said I did well and showed lots of character, which meant a lot to me.

The boxing season finished in line with school, but I kept training by running every couple of nights. I was out jogging one night in the dark and this car pulled up alongside me on the main road. The passenger window went down, and the driver leant over and asked me for some directions. I told him and said it wasn't far.

He said, "Do you think anyone there would be interested in these sex magazines?"

I replied, "I don't know."

He then said, "Why don't you jump in and have a look at them with me?"

I said, "Fuck off," and I hastily ran off.

When I got home, I felt sick in my stomach. As I got older, I realised there were nasty people all over the place, and London had plenty of perverts.

That summer we moved to a council flat in a nineteen-storey tower block in West London. I didn't mind as West London had loads of history, with the Mods and the rock band called the Who coming from there. Also, there were loads of shops and a market with several tube stations, all within a five-minute walk. There was also the BBC headquarters and other BBC buildings all around the area.

One night I was waiting to catch a bus to go to see a friend. Several bus stops were not far apart along the main road, and I stood back from them beside a large BBC theatre and a large cinema building. There was an alleyway between the two buildings. This bloke approached me and said, "Would you like to earn some money, son?"

I replied, "What doing?" and he said, "Come down the alleyway, and I'll show you." Luckily, my bus just pulled up to the stop at that moment, and I ran over and jumped on it. Fucking pervert.

I couldn't wait to get back in the boxing gym, and we went to many boxing shows at places like Kings Cross Town Hall, Manor Place Baths, West Ham working men's club, York Hall Bethnal Green, Municipal Hall Tottenham, Neasden Town Hall, Acton Town Hall, Battersea Town Hall, Clarendon Hotel Hammersmith, Guinness Social Club in Park Royal, and many other boxing clubs that held their shows in their own gym.

I had a mixture of results – some good, some bad. Sometimes I underperformed and other times I was robbed by the judges. On other occasions I was at my very best and I felt invincible. In my first proper competition, the *Feds* (the federation of boys' clubs), I lost at York Hall Bethnal Green, East London on a split decision (majority) to a kid from Thamesmead, South London. I had what looked like a love bite on my shoulder, where he had bitten me with his gumshield in. It was all part of learning the boxing game.

My next competition was the schoolboys boxing championships. I became Middlesex champion, then home counties champion, then in the quarter-finals of the national schoolboys I beat a boxer from Plymouth, Devon. In the crowd was a famous professional boxing trainer from Chatteris, Cambridge, whose son was in a bout. He had two of his professional fighters there in support for his son, Joe Bugner and Dave 'Boy' Green. We got to shake their hands. I stopped the boy from Plymouth in the second round, so I was pleased they got to see me perform well.

In the national semi-finals, I came up against a real tough lad from Essex, whose brother boxed for England. This lad had won every one of his fights by stoppage, and I had never been stopped. It was going to be a great contest, and it turned out to be just that. The noise was deafening from the crowd as we knocked the shit out of each other. I lost a majority points decision, and I had my jaw dislocated. My trainer just yanked it back into position, and I got this searing pain inside my ear, like someone had put a hot needle into it. The other lad went on to win by a stoppage in the national final and became the UK champion. I was proud to be the only boy he couldn't stop, but my jaw still clicks today. Next up were the Junior ABAs in March. I won the northwest divisional title, known as *The Divs*.

In London we had four divisions, NW, SW, NE, and SE. You had to win your divisional title, which sometimes entail up to three fights in one night. I only ever had two in one night; it depended on how many boys had entered at your weight category. The four divisional champions would then meet in the semi-finals, after a draw was made on the night. This semi-finals night was at Battersea Town Hall. I got drawn to fight the SW champion, who was the favourite to win.

The feeling before you get into a boxing ring in front of hundreds of people can be overwhelming and extremely nervous. No matter how tough you may be, you will feel sick with nerves. There were still a few bouts to go before my fight. I decided to have a cup of tea with lots of sugar in it; they also had slices of brown bread pudding with sugar sprinkled on top for ten pence. I thought, *Why not?*

I was halfway through the bread pudding slice and the tea when my trainer came rushing up to me and said, "Come on, Roger, you're on next." There had been a couple of fights stopped early, and I had to quickly get gloved up and head to the ring, only seconds after eating my bread pudding. The other kid came at me like a train and caught me early with some good punches. I rallied a bit at the end of the first round, and it was even when I sat on my stool. The second round started, and again he was on me like a shot. To this day I do not know where this came from, but I had him on the ropes and I let go two stinging left jabs in quick succession. He just sat on the bottom rope and fell out of the ring onto the judges' table. He was out cold. What a win against one of the best boys in the UK. I told my trainer afterwards, "It was the bread pudding."

At the Junior ABA London Final at Battersea Town Hall a week later, I fought the NE divisional champion. I won a unanimous decision on points to be the new Light-Welterweight Junior ABA London champion. My father and brothers were there cheering me on and congratulating me afterwards. They wanted to go out partying, but I just wanted to go home to show my trophy to my mother. I ached all over, and I had rope burns across my back, and both of my thumbs had swollen up, bruised and sore. I left Battersea and got onto the bus to go home. Being in South London, this meant the bus went across one of the bridges over the river Thames. I was sitting upstairs on the bus in the back seat.

The bus was empty, and it was about 11:00 p.m. This Jamaican bus conductor came up the stairs to take my fare, looking out of the window at all the buildings and lights shining on the river Thames as we drove over it. I said to him, "You see out there? That's London, and I'm the champion of all of it." He just smiled and said, "Of course you are, son. Of course you are," and he went down the stairs smiling shaking his head. But I knew I was the champion of London – it was 'my' city.

I fought next in the National ABA semi-finals. It was an all-day affair as there were so many different age categories and boys from all over the UK there. Because we were local and we didn't have too far to travel, I was going to be one of the last contests, which made the day even longer as we couldn't go anywhere, just stay and watch the other bouts.

I was drawn against the reigning Junior ABA champion, who was six feet tall. I spent the whole fight chasing him around the ring; he was just so good at jab and move, jab and move. I finally caught him in the third round, but right at the end – it was a left hook that sent him to the floor. He would not have beaten the count of ten, but the bell went to end the fight. His trainers got into the ring and helped him up and to a stool in his corner.

We went to the centre of the ring with the ref holding each of our arms while we waited for the decision. It was a majority win for him, two judges to one. I was disappointed but not surprised. I had hardly laid a glove on him for the first two rounds. My trainers and family were very angry and thought I should have got the decision due to the way it ended. It seemed to happen a lot throughout my boxing career, as I was a box fighter and not a classic boxer, which meant I took a few punches before returning with more of my own. The classic rule of boxing is hit and don't be hit, but that was never very exciting for me.

On my seventeenth birthday, I became a senior boxer and could now fight other boxers of any age i.e., grown men. My first senior bout was against a man from a good North London club. He was a policeman and twenty-six years old. Policemen have it tough, as any boxer does not need any encouragement, to give his all when up against a policeman and especially with it being legal to hit them in a boxing ring, and I was no different. He was a tough opponent, though, and he had gone unshaven for days, rubbing the stubble from his chin into my baby face, causing it to go red and sore. The sweat ran down my face and over my red, raw skin, stinging like mad. Welcome to boxing against adults. It was a real battle, with me winning a unanimous decision on points.

Three weeks later, at the end of November 1977, I boxed in the London Feds Semi-final at York Hall Bethnal Green, East London, against a boy from Fisher Boxing Club, South London. He was called Lloyd Honeyghan. He came into the ring, and he was a little taller than me, but not by much, he had black-and-white shorts covered in badges, and a green, yellow, and red tassel hanging from the shorts. He was Jamaican with a pretty-boy face. I thought, *Okay, let's get it on.* What I wasn't expecting was his hand speed; he was like lightning with both hands, and he certainly hit me often enough. I sat down on the stool at the end of the first round, and my trainer said, "Well done, Rog. He's hardly laid a glove on you."

I replied, "Well, watch the ref, then, as someone is hitting me."

Whenever I met my trainers over the later years throughout my life, they always reminded me of what I said. They thought it very funny. I went on to lose a majority points decision to Lloyd Honeyghan, who went on to win the NABC national title. In 1986, as a professional, he would be British, Commonwealth, European, and undisputed World Welterweight Champion. I congratulate him, as he achieved something I could never have achieved, and he will be in the history books forever.

In March 1978 at the Municipal Hall, Tottenham, I won the Senior ABA Northwest London divisional title. This now made me an 'open class' boxer, i.e., one who has won a senior title. Usually we boxed three two-minute rounds, but as an open-class boxer and in the Senior ABAs, we'd box three three-minute rounds, and you could only box against other open-class boxers or intermediate boxers. (In other words, those that had boxed in the ABAs but had lost and not won any titles.)

The London ABA semi-finals were held at Seymour Baths in Marylebone, a stone's throw away from Paddington in West London. I fought a very good boxer who was the SE divisional champion. It was a real battle, and I honestly couldn't remember much after he hit me in the middle of the first round, with a classic straight left punch. (He was a southpaw, which meant he led with a right jab, then banged hard with his left, opposite to me, as I was an orthodox boxer leading with the left jab.)

I finally understood what they mean by 'seeing stars' – everything was white and hazy for the rest of the fight. I could see him and the ref, but everything behind them seemed white. There were little flickers of light, like if you've looked at a light bulb too long. I got a majority decision in my favour, which was very unusual for me. That meant I was now going to box at the Royal Albert Hall, Kensington, in the Senior Light-Welterweight London ABA final, just twelve months after winning the same title as a junior boxer.

I was going to box an England boxer from East London. He was the young England captain, and they said he'd had over one hundred bouts, losing just a couple from when he was very young. He was eighteen years old, and I was seventeen years old. He had won everything as a junior but at the weight below, as a lightweight. It's amazing when two people who have been living parallel lives, equally harsh, who have developed boxing skills to go with their hard characters, then come face to face for the first time across a boxing ring. This is what makes boxing such a unique sport.

Everyone in amateur boxing was licking their lips at the thought of us two meeting at the Royal Albert Hall in front of two thousand people. It would be fair to say at this time he was No. 1 Light-Welterweight in the UK, with me at No. 3. The day arrived, and I had gone to the club gym to have a trial weigh-in. I had been really struggling to keep down to ten stone in weight (light-welterweight) for the past two years.

I hadn't eaten for two days, other than some lettuce leaves and slices of ham and cucumber, with no liquids whatsoever. I didn't feel very strong, I can tell you. I weighed a bit over the limit, so I had to put on a plastic sweat suit and skip it off over the next thirty or forty minutes. Not ideal on the morning of the biggest fight of your life, but it was still a long time until I'd be stepping into the ring that night.

We arrived at the Royal Albert Hall in the afternoon to do the official weigh-in and for me to have a medical. My trainer pointed to one of the mansion flats opposite and said, "Benny Hill lives there." I thought that was funny, and I wondered if he was indoors writing comedy sketches at this time of the day. I got on the scales just in my underpants and I was bang on ten stone – what a relief. That meant I could now eat as it was still quite a few hours until I was boxing.

I was sitting around the dressing rooms when I picked up a London evening newspaper. There was a preview piece written in there about tonight's Senior London ABA finals. My heart sank when it said, "Watch out for the hard-hitting East London star, who has conquered all before him over the last four years as a top junior and is now looking to add his first senior title. I was in Canning Town at Terry Lawless's gym this week, and I saw him give the World Lightweight Champion, Jim Watt, a gruelling six rounds of sparring. This kid is something special."

With as much bravado as I could muster, I thought, *I'll show him who's something special when I win the London title*, but I was just kidding myself really. How could I compete with that? He's sparring with a world-professional boxing champ at one of the most famous gyms in the world. Training there were world champs Jim Watt, John H. Stracey, and Maurice Hope, and the gym would go on to have future champs like Frank Bruno, Lloyd Honeyghan, and many others, and there I was just sparring with other lads like me in our amateur gym. We were miles apart.

The time had come to leave the changing rooms and head up the stairs to the main hall. As I looked up, I could see trumpets sticking out with coats of arms hanging from them; the noise was deafening from the trumpets. As I got level with the floor of the main hall, a very bright light suddenly hit me in the face. I could just see all the seats and the darkness, with this lit-up boxing ring that looked a mile away in the distance. My legs felt like jelly and my stomach was doing somersaults, but I was thinking over and over in my head, *you're here because you want to be here – you deserve to be here.* The crowd was applauding as I walked with my trainers to the ring. I got through the ropes, and my opponent was already in the other corner.

Then the lights all went on. I stood completely amazed at this circular building. I looked around at all the private boxes with little lights from the cigarette lighters dotting about as people lit up their cigs. The MC started to make the announcements. I knew all about my opponent's power in both hands, and his left hook to the body was probably his best punch. My best punch was a sharp straight left jab that I could use to get myself in and out quite well.

As soon as we got going, he was reading my jabs expertly and sinking in those hard body shots into my ribs every time I threw a jab. In the end I stopped throwing them; he had taken away my best punch. The first round ended with the score even, and my trainer said to me whilst I was on the stool, "Try to feint a jab, then throw two quick ones." I nodded, but I felt very weak. He won the second round, and then he stepped up the tempo in the third round.

I had no answers to his skill and hooks to the body, and due to all the weight loss, both of my legs cramped up at the backs of both thighs. I was moving around like the Frankenstein monster. I took everything he could throw at me and remained on my feet, but with just ten seconds left of the last round, the ref gave me a standing eight count, then waved his arms to stop the contest. I complained, but he said it was for my own good. It was the first time I had ever been stopped in a boxing ring. I was gutted, but I knew in my heart he was better than me.

Many years later my trainers told me, "We should have let you go up a weight and missed the ABAs that year. You could have entered the following year at eighteen and at welterweight." But it doesn't matter now – it's all water under the bridge. I have loads to thank everyone at the club for; my trainers were like fathers to me, and I learnt so much from them about life, as well as boxing.

In the summer break, I called my trainer, Tony, up and told him I was going to turn professional. He asked me not to, as he said, "You are good, Roger, but not that good. You should only turn professional if you think you can win things and be the best. I don't think you are that good to do that. I've seen too many boxers get ruined in the professionals and end up punch drunk. I don't want that to happen to you, Roger." Talk about an honest answer.

Tony was always as straight a man as you could find – no messing. I thought about what he said, but I felt an urge to give it a go. I knew a few other boxing managers wanted me to turn pro with them, but Terry Lawless was my preferred choice in Canning Town. I left my flat and got the tube all the way to West Ham Station on the Metropolitan line, a journey from West to East London. I arrived at the gym, which was above a pub called the Royal Oak, Canning Town. I went upstairs to the gym, and Mr Lawless's assistant, Frank Black, was there getting things ready as the boxers started arriving. I sat down on this box-type bench that ran along the wall under the large windows. Outside the window I was looking on to the roof of the red buses that terminated in the lay-by outside the pub.

Charlie Magri was the first boxer to come in. He came over beside me and put his boot up onto the bench beside me doing the laces up.

"You come to turn pro, have you?" he said in a very East London cockney accent.

I replied, "Yes, I am waiting to see Mr Lawless."

Other boxers started to come in, like Jimmy Batten British, light-middleweight champion; John L. Gardner British, heavyweight champion; and a couple of others, including an old boxing friend of mine from Kilburn. Mr Lawless came in, took off his jacket, and rolled up his white shirtsleeves. He came over to me and said, "How are you doing? You'd like to turn professional, then?"

I replied that I thought he would be the best manger to turn professional with, and I'd like to give it a go. He was very polite and explained to me that he currently had too many boxers on his books at my weight, and he would not be able to fit me in. He suggested that I go over to another boxing gym in Lavender Hill, Clapham, South London. He even said he would give them a call for me, as he knew they were looking for new boxers. I thanked him and asked, "Now that I'm here, can I train a bit?"

He said, "Of course. Go and get yourself changed, and you can do some bag work and a bit of skipping."

I got changed and joined in with the other boxers. I felt like a professional boxer. Whilst I was on the punch bag, I was taking it all in with the smells I knew so well. When I got changed and I was just leaving the changing room, the lad I had lost to at the Royal Albert Hall came in. We just nodded to each other; he didn't turn professional for another year. I went home on the tube thinking about what my trainer had said, and my father had also said that I should finish my apprenticeship before turning professional, therefore I would at least have a trade to fall back on if I wasn't successful as a professional boxer. Mr Lawless's nice words were also going through my head. I came to the conclusion that I wouldn't go over to Lavender Hill Clapham; I would finish my apprenticeship, then see how I felt, because if Mr Lawless didn't want me, I wasn't going to anyone else, as he was the best, and maybe Tony was right. Maybe I was good but not that good.

After that summer of 1978, I returned to training in September at eleven stone – light-middleweight – and yet there was not an ounce of fat on me. I never got to box at welterweight, and being an open class boxer, I could only fight other top open class boxers, which made the one-stone rise in weight even tougher. It's fair to say I wasn't as good at the higher weight. I did represent the London ABA team a couple of times, though, the most notable being against the army at a large camp up north somewhere. We were winning about 6–0 when I got in the ring. I was up against a very good boxer who had got to the ABA final a year earlier. I didn't start off too well, and he battered me for the first two rounds; he was an excellent boxer. The crowd was right behind him as they sensed their first win of the night. I was on the ropes halfway through the last round under a deluge of punches, when out of nowhere I produced a right uppercut that caught him under his chin. His face went onto my left shoulder, I stepped to one side, and he fell face first to the canvass – out cold. What a relief, and a great win out of nowhere. I was very lucky. The crowd wasn't very happy, but the other London lads were overjoyed.

I would go on to pull back from boxing, and I stopped for several months now and again, as I drifted away from the sport and grew older with other priorities in my life. I did go to other pro gyms to train, where I enjoyed the atmosphere and sparred hundreds of rounds with different boxers that you would call journeymen who 'had boots will travel' as their personal mantra. They were tough men, not the best of boxers, but they were earning £1,000 a month boxing anyone, mostly up-and-coming young professionals who needed to use them as stepping stones at the start of their professional apprenticeships. I remember one of these boxers had a record of seventy fights with four wins, two draws, and sixty-four losses, but when I sparred with him, he was a very hard and tough man to box against. He hurt you with his elbows, shoulders, and head. Unfortunately, like most of the journeymen, he was easy to hit.

Chapter Five
Leaving School

Before leaving school in our last year, I remember there was a male teacher that one of our friends had some trouble with. He really did not like him. There was a real clash of personalities, and the teacher kept picking on him all the time. Every day this teacher would drive into the school car park with a pretty female teacher sitting beside him, in his little old soft-top sports car. My mates decided to attack the teacher's car and sliced through the canvass roof several times with a knife and slashed the tyres. (I had left school early on this day, as I was boxing that night.) What they didn't know was the car belonged to the female teacher, but she let him drive her to school in it. Our friend got expelled from school; the others were suspended.

Shortly after this we were out at a disco club, and when we were leaving the club around 1:00 a.m., all hell broke out and we were attacked by this group of punk rockers. Our friend who had been expelled had beaten up one of these punks a week earlier, and they wanted revenge. I somehow got separated from the main group, and I was now fighting two punk rockers on my own. I could see my mates on the other side of the punks, throwing bottles at them that had been left in a crate in a shop doorway. I was kicking the punk who was on the floor in front of me, and his mate was punching me in the back, but I couldn't feel much as I was busy keeping this other one on the floor.

Suddenly the punk behind me started to kick his mate on the floor saying, "Get the fucking knife out." I turned and hit the punk behind me, then ran down the road. I wasn't hanging about if knives were involved. They were both now chasing after me, and I saw the shine off the knife. I went around a corner and jumped over a small wall and lay under a hedge in the front garden. They both went running past, and after a while I made my way back to my friend's house nearby, where I was going to be staying the night. My friends were already there, and we had a good laugh about it all. We were only sixteen, but we were growing up fast.

In your last year at school, it is important to have an idea of what sort of career you would be best suited to, or what you think you would enjoy doing for the rest of your life. The butcher shop had offered me an apprenticeship to work full time at the shop and become a qualified butcher, or I could work on the building sites as a labourer or train to get a trade. I also loved photography. Throughout my final year at school, I did not participate in games. I had spoken with my art teacher, who was a photography enthusiast, and he spoke with the games teacher, who agreed that due to me training five nights a week and a Sunday morning for my boxing, and also playing football for the school team, I could be excused from the games lessons.

In place of games I did photography, even though it was only meant for sixth formers. I had also joined a private photography evening class that met once a week above a shop in Moorgate. I really enjoyed developing my own photographs and looking for the different and the unusual with a camera. As all the kids at school went to games, I would walk out of the school and walk along the Grand Union Canal, and anywhere else I thought I could get a good picture. I'd go back to the school and go into the darkroom in the art class and develop the photographs I had just taken. They were black and white.

By the end of the year, I had covered the whole syllabus for the photography O level. I needed to get this as I wanted to get an A-level in art and photography that would get me into the Harrow College of Art to study for a BA degree in photography and art. However, our headmaster had other ideas. He refused to allow me to take the O level in photography, and he said it was only for sixth formers and I would have to stay on and do it a year later.

That's when I decided to become a bricklayer instead. I left school at the end of June in 1977, with two O levels and seven CSEs. I didn't need the exams as I had already been offered a bricklaying apprenticeship with the large main contractor called John Laing & Sons Ltd. I had interviews and tests and was offered apprenticeships with Laing's, Taylor Woodrow, and Wimpey's, but I chose Laing's, as my father said they were the best for bricklaying. I left school on the Friday and started my bricklaying apprenticeship on Monday 4 July 1977.

This happened because at the interview, the John Laing apprentice training officer was very impressed that I had worked on building sites from the age of thirteen with my brother-in-law. He said I could start early in July, whereas the other apprentices would not start until college started in September. There I was on the Monday morning up at 6:00 a.m. and off to work for my first day as a bricklaying apprentice. I had bought a set of bricklaying tools from a store in the market, and I was sitting on a tube going to Edgware Road Station where I had to get off and walk through Chapel Street market up towards St John's Wood to the building site. I was to report to the general foreman.

The GF was about sixty years old, and he'd spent his whole working life at John Laing. He was a fantastic man and taught me so much. It was strange on that first day with the other bricklayers of all ages taking the piss out of me and my new tool bag. They rummaged through my new tools, throwing some of them out saying, "You won't need that, and you won't need one of them." I just laughed and told them to fuck off. I fitted in straight away. I spent two months on the site learning what I could from the bricklayers, who were all great fun to be around. I had my own past experiences with Kevin to recall, and my father coming from the civil engineering background of tunnelling and roads. It all helped me not to be too scared of the building site environment.

I thought it was very funny being with men older than my father but being treated the same, like in the site canteen at tea breaks, one of the old fellas would hold up a newspaper showing a page 3 model saying, "Look at the tits on her," and everyone laughing, with me just blushing and smiling innocently.

On one day there was a bad accident. The party walls between the flats we were building were nine inches thick. We were using a new brick that was like two bricks joined together to make it a full nine inches wide. It was called a Calculon brick and new to the market. A normal brick was just four and a half inches wide. The tower crane started to lift a pallet load of Calculon bricks up and over our heads, and as it lowered them, the bottom of the pallet caught the top of a long scaffold tube that was sticking up in the air, tipping the pallet of bricks. The safety net hadn't been fastened properly, and the 450 bricks came raining down. Luckily, I was about fifty feet away and not in any danger, but I remember one of the hod carriers running and all the bricks landing on the backs of his legs as he dived to the ground. He was in a bad way as all the bricklayers scrambled to get all the bricks off him. He was taken away in an ambulance, with badly damaged legs. I never heard what happened to him, but he never came back to work.

We had this real character on the site named 'Three in the Bed' Syd. He got his nickname because, apparently, he had sex with his wife and their eighteen-year-old female lodger at the same time. He was about forty-five years old and a bit of a pervert. He used to show blue cine films in the changing rooms during lunch breaks, charging the men fifty pence a time to enter. He wouldn't let me in as he said I was too young. He also stole things from the site, as he was building an extension to his house. He had this old canvass bag that he would put one concrete block into each night and take it home. He had been doing this for months, and the weight of the block and its sharp edges had worn an outline in the bag, so you could see the shape of the block in the bag.

There was a bit of an enquiry on the site one Monday morning, as he had tried to steal a large T-type diesel cement mixer over the weekend from the site. When they finished work at 1:00 p.m. on Saturday, he hooked the mixer to the back of his old Land Rover and drove off with it, but as he went around the first corner the mixer tipped over and crashed to the road onto its side. He got out unhooked it and just drove away, leaving it in the middle of the road. The police were on the site on Monday, but no one said anything, and he got away with it.

I loved listening to the bricklayers' stories. One of the bricklayers had been working on a house in East Acton (beside Shepherd's Bush) in 1966 when he heard gunshots and screeching tyres from farther along the road. He looked up from the scaffolding and he saw a car speeding away from another stationary car. The shooter had just shot two policemen, and his mate had shot a third – the policemen all died. The men were eventually caught and spent the next four decades in prison.

My boxing trainers Tony and Sam used to tell me lots of stories about two East London gangsters who were twins. One time my trainers were drinking in a pub in Paddington in the early sixties when Tony said he noticed a few new faces he hadn't seen before. He could tell from their accents they were from East London. One of Tony's friends, Jamie, had bumped into one of these East Londoners spilling his beer. The bloke turned around and knocked Jamie out onto the floor, so Tony, who had a great left hook from his boxing days, knocked the East Londoner spark out with one punch. It all calmed down, and about an hour later the twins entered the pub. It all went quiet and one of them said, "Who is the bloke with the good left hook, then?" I thought Tony was going to say they had a right tear up with them, but he didn't. He said, "We went straight out the side door and got on our toes and got away sharpish." A boxing friend of mine has an uncle who worked as a driver for the twins for a couple of years. He told me he used to just drive and say nothing – that was his job. He explained to the twins that he was getting married and he wanted to settle down to a more normal life, and they gave him some money and wished him well.

I had to leave all the men at the site in September and attend college for six months. I had really enjoyed my two months, and I felt like a proper John Laing's man. I could also lay bricks. On my first day at college in northwest London, I met about twenty-five other bricklaying apprentices. Only one of them was working for John Laing; the others were mostly from some smaller companies. They were just boys to me. Can you imagine the difference between me and them, and the lives we had lived? They had left school in July and had done nothing for two months. This was their first day apprenticing. I had been working on sites at weekends and in the summer holidays since I was thirteen years old, and then I had two months on a large John Laing's site as an apprentice bricklayer. The difference between us was huge, and it made my life very easy.

After the six months at college, myself and the other Laing apprentice were placed on a site in Acton. This was about two miles from where I lived. The Acton housing site was a vast mixture of houses and flats in a very nice red brick with black mortar and raked-out joints. You had to be a very good bricklayer to lay them cleanly. I spent twenty months of my apprenticeship on this site, and I loved every minute of it. Don't forget I was boxing at this time as well, and many of the men from the site would come to the shows to watch me fight. In my second year I was chosen by John Laing's head office as best apprentice of the year in the London region. This was a great accolade to win, and all the brickies were pleased, as for the previous three years a carpenter apprentice had won it.

Whilst on the Acton site a year later, I was asked by the site manager if I would like to appear in a TV programme on BBC 1 called *Going to Work*. It was designed for school leavers to see what sort of people did what sort of jobs, to help them choose a career path. I said yes and spent three days with a BBC film crew filming. They filmed me laying bricks, talking in the site canteen to an interviewer, having a driving lesson, and at the boys' club where they filmed me training and sparring. They also came to our flat and filmed all of my trophies from boxing. Whilst filming me running through Shepherd's Bush Green in my tracksuit with bandaged hands, I heard an onlooker say, "Is that Bodie from the professionals?" That made me smile.

The BBC film crew were very nice, and you could tell they were very experienced. They invited all of us who were in the programme to a tour of the BBC headquarters. We saw them filming *Playschool*, *Blue Peter*, and a quiz show about Europe with two teams of three celebrities. I only recognised James Hunt, the racing driver, and the quiz host was Robert Robinson. It was fascinating to see what happened in the old BBC headquarters. They told me the most expensive thing in all the studios was the floor, as it had to be perfectly level for the large cameras to move over without any movements, and the floors were renewed every year with a liquid screed. They took us upstairs to the BBC bar, roof garden, and canteen. It was funny seeing people still in full period costume queueing up to pay for their ham roll and coffee in the canteen; it made me laugh.

After all the filming ended, I was asked by John Laing's if I'd like to be in their latest promotional magazine that got sent out to clients and to attract new trainees to the company. I said yes, and I was then photographed at work and interviewed about my apprenticeship and how great John Laing's were. I still have the magazine and a DVD of the programme *Going to Work* that anyone can view on YouTube.

It seemed that in 1978/79, I was surrounded by film crews. Every day I'd travel back and forth to the Acton site, and a couple of times I looked down from the top of the bus whilst going along Goldhawk Road near to Shepherd's Bush market, and I would see a film crew with lights on stands all around them filming. There would be a couple of blokes in black leather with motorbikes. Then the next time I saw them it was outside the supermarket on the opposite side of Goldhawk Road, filming a bloke in a green parker jacket, talking to an attractive blond girl. I was told by one of the blokes on the site, they were filming a mod movie called *Quadrophenia*, written by the Who. I saw the film when it came out. It was great, but you didn't see me on the bus, though, which was disappointing. Only kidding.

Whilst on the Acton site, I also had to attend a technical college one day and one evening each week. I didn't mind college, as it was all about the technical side of brickwork that I enjoyed and the practical that I was very good at. I passed my City & Guilds in bricklaying with a distinction in the theory and a credit in the practical and another credit in the exam paper. My lecturer at college told me to pick up a bit on the practical in the following year, as I could then get two distinctions that would mean being awarded a Silver Trowel, which was very coveted and not many people got them. I did as he said, but alas my theory went backwards a bit. I ended up in the advanced City & Guilds with a distinction in my practical and two credits in the theory work and exam, and no Silver Trowel.

John Laing's eventually transferred me from Acton to a project in Wapping, East London. I had passed my driving test by this time and thought if I left early enough, I could drive straight along the embankment by the river Thames to Tower Bridge and then along the old highway to Wapping. I left my flat at 6:15 a.m. and arrived at the site about 7:15 a.m. I didn't start work until 8:00 a.m., so I went into the canteen and spoke to some of the men. They pointed me in the direction of this huge man who was the general foreman. It was pouring rain and still dark, with mud everywhere – not a very welcoming place.

I walked up behind this GF as he was directing a forklift truck that was unloading a lorry full of large glass windows. I heard this shouting, then this almighty crash! All the large glass windows hit the ground and smashed. All the men came running out of the canteen. The GF shouted many swear words at the forklift truck driver, then he pulled open the truck door, and we thought he was going to hit the driver, but the driver just fell out of the cab and onto the muddy ground in the rain. He was as drunk as a skunk and could barely stand up. There was a large plastic lemonade bottle in the cab full of neat vodka. The driver got up and legged it off the site. What a start on my first day. I hated it there. Everything was so dark and dreary and just rough – and I mean very rough. The brickwork was being slung up by cowboys, who had just returned from making shed loads of money in Germany. There had been a boom in building work in Germany, and many men went over there as labourers and returned as bricklayers. They made a TV programme about it called *Auf Wiedersehen, Pet.*

My first car was a Mark III Ford Cortina, and after a couple of months I noticed it needed a new wing as one of the front wings was rusting at a fast rate. I went over to a local scrapyard to see if they had any old Ford Cortinas in. I was lucky as he had a couple ready to be crushed. He told me to go and take the wing off of one of them, which I did, then he said, "That'll be £20, young man." I paid him and fitted the wing to my car and sprayed it yellow. For an eighteen-year-old, I thought I did quite a good job. Then the clutch went on the car – that I couldn't do. I bought a replacement clutch from the scrapyard, and one of my brothers did the job.

I took it out to go to a friend's house, but as I was sitting at the red traffic light on Shepherd's Bush Green heading for Wood Lane, it changed to green, and as I put the car into gear, the gear lever came away in my hand. I panicked and didn't know what to do. There was a big red bus behind me that nearly hit the back of my car, as the driver thought I would move forwards after the lights changed. He was blaring away on his horn, so I got out and I held up the gear lever and said, "What do you expect me to do?" He just laughed, and he got out and helped me to stick the lever back in, and to get the car across the junction and into a side road. My brother sorted it out the next day. I had broken the circlip, releasing the gear lever. It was my fault. I decided to get rid of the car and manage without one for a while. After all, in London you can manage with the tube, buses, or walking.

I had heard about these new machines just coming out called video recorders. I saw one advertised in my local paper for sale at £450. I contacted the seller, and it was a man who was the local MP for my area. He explained he bought it new, thinking he could record things on TV that he would otherwise miss due to working long hours, but after a month he found he wasn't getting the time to watch the recordings, so he gave up and hence he was now selling it. I went home with my new toy very excited. What I didn't realise was that it was a Betamax top loader machine, and most of the new videotapes starting to arrive in the shops were VHS and not Betamax. A completely different type altogether. There weren't many shops stocking Betamax videotapes, so I had to go to Tottenham Court Road or Edgware Road to find them in the electrical shops. I had a great tape of an Elvis comeback special, where he was dressed all in black leather, and they had a studio audience sitting around him and the musicians in a circle. I recorded *Top of the Pops* every week, but after a couple of months I got fed up with it and I sold the video recorder.

I bought another Mark III Ford Cortina. I wasn't having much luck with cars, and I came down from our high-rise flat one morning to drive to work, and my car wasn't there. I was sure I had parked it in my usual place down one of the quiet side roads, but it had gone. It's a bizarre feeling as you walk around all the adjoining roads scratching your head. You go over parking it in your mind a hundred times. After about an hour, I gave up and headed to the police station to report it stolen. My bricklaying tools were in the boot as well, which was very annoying. I bought an old Hillman Hunter car from the local paper for £200 as a quick replacement. After three weeks, it started making a knocking sound. My brother had a look at it and said, "The big ends are going, you better get rid of it." It was very funny, as the key barrel was loose in it, and you had to twist the keys whilst twisting the barrel in a certain way to get it started. I got it to a South London car auction, and I told the auctioneer to put it through for £250. I eagerly waited for my car to be the next to be driven in for the auction bids to begin.

Wouldn't you know it, the idiots out the back couldn't get it to start, even though I had shown them several times how to start it. Two blokes pushed the car into the sales area, and another bloke was steering it. I only got £150 for it.

A week later I got a message from the police station. They had found my stolen car. The bad news was they said it was undriveable. I went to the address in NW London where it had been dumped in a side road. I was expecting to see it written off or smashed up a bit, but it was all okay, apart from where the locals, who once they realised it was a stolen car and dumped by joy riders, and not owned by anyone in their road, had been helping themselves. My quadrophonic stereo system, the headlights, hubcaps, and even my furry dice were gone, the thieving bastards! The reason it was undriveable was they had also nicked the battery. I managed to get it home by the weekend, and I did it all up a bit and got it back driving once again after a few more visits to the scrapyard.

Around this period, I bumped into an old friend I hadn't seen for a couple of years. I had just managed to squeeze in between the shutting tube doors on the last train from Baker Street. I had been out for the night with friends in Kingsbury, near Wembley, and I had to change trains at Baker Street. I sat down and this old friend came and sat beside me. He had been away in Borstal. He had a few drops of blood on his clothes. He told me how he had come out of a pub in Queensbury called the Queen of Hearts, and this bloke had confronted him and tried to mug him. He pulled out a knife to show it to me, and it still had blood on it. He said, "I stuck him twice, then legged it all the way to the tube station." I thought, *Great, if we get collared by the law now, I'll be his accomplice.* I asked him where he was going, and he said, "They've got me holed up in a hostel in Shepherd's Bush." We got off the train together, and I said, "I live in the opposite direction to you," and I got away from him very quickly.

After working for about six weeks in Wapping, they transferred me to the famous Barbican Centre, beside Moorgate and Liverpool Street. The whole Barbican area was the largest building development in Europe. John Laing's started it in 1958 and initially had to move a large graveyard and kill many wild cats that had made it their home, beside a small church where Oliver Cromwell got married. They built two or three big tower blocks of flats and a lot of low-level dwellings, a road tunnel, and then the iconic arts centre, which was mostly underground, although it had a massive glass atrium up on the roof for exotic flowers and trees, and over beside London Wall was a manmade lake with circular pond features alongside all in circular brickwork.

One of their biggest challenges on the project was when decimalisation came in 1970/71. All the dimensions on the drawings had to be changed, and believe me, on a project of this size, there were hundreds of drawings, and some were very complex. Then they had all the imperial-size bricks that were now of no use, as the new dimensions had to incorporate the new metric-size bricks. There were over a thousand workers on site when I turned up to start my first day. I found the general foreman. He seemed like the no nonsense type of man, who looked me up and down, then looked through my tool bag and said, "Okay, come with me for a walk first."

I must add that this GF had been on this project since it started, and that was a very long time to be on the same site – twenty-one years. He had gone past retirement age and was sixty-six years old. John Laing had said he could stay on until it was finished. The men called him Mr Barbican. We began our walk around the site, and he said, "You will not see finer workmanship anywhere in the world than what you see on this project." I noticed a brick tipping on the wall we walked past. I said, "Well, that's not very good – that brick is tipping." He shouted, "What? How dare you criticise the work, and you just out of nappies!" Not the best of starts by me, and I quickly apologised.

I was there for six months and finished my apprenticeship on this famous construction project. It was opened by the Queen in 1980. I saw it on the TV news, and there was the GF in dickie bow and black dinner suit shaking hands with the Queen. Well done, sir. Many years later, I went back to visit the theatre to watch *Antony and Cleopatra*. I sat in the audience and looked up high above the stage, where the fire curtain was, and I remembered as a young apprentice cutting out bricks from a tower scaffold right there above where the stage would be.

In 1978 I went on my first solo holiday. There was this small cabin at the entrance to a local tube station that sold cheap holidays for the people under twenty-six. I bought a return ticket to Athens, Greece, for £40 on a coach. I told my parents I was going on a guided coach tour, so they wouldn't worry about me, but I was just going on my own. I got on the coach at Hanover Square, just off Regent Street in the West End. I remembered my mother saying during the war she was a spotter on top of an office building in Hanover Square, which made it a strange feeling for me looking up to the buildings' roofs in 1978. I imagined what it must have been like thirty-four years earlier right there. This coach service that travelled cheaply around Europe was nicknamed the *Magic*

Bus as lots of hippies would use them, and they would be full of smoke from them smoking weed. It took two and a half days to get to Athens via France, Switzerland, Italy, and Yugoslavia. We entered northern Greece at Salonica, then went down the coast road to Athens. We passed through Paris, Lyon, Geneva, Torino, Milan, Venice, Zagreb, Belgrade, Salonica, then Athens. I loved every minute of it, except when we got to Geneva, Switzerland, and the driver announced we would be stopping to pick up some survivors from an earlier coach that had crashed in the Alps. I shit myself. They were very dangerous coaches driving through the night, and the Greek drivers would swap at the wheel of the moving coach, in the mountains.

I had a great time in Athens in the heat. I loved seeing the Acropolis, the changing of the guard, a museum of the very first Olympic Games, and several of the Greek islands. Aegina, Syros, Serifos, and Kythnos were all very uncommercial and quiet in 1978. I ate octopus for the first time; it just tasted like salty rubber to me. I enjoyed Syntagma Square and the flea market, which reminded me of markets in London. It was the first time I had experienced temperatures above a hundred degrees.

The following Easter break saw me travelling once again, as I saw it as a great way to get out of London on an adventure. I bought a ferry ticket to Ostend, Belgium. When I got there, I got a train to Brussels. It seemed like a nice place with lots of tree-lined roads. I then saw this train in the station going to Luxembourg. I got on it. When we arrived in Luxembourg, I was laughing to myself, as I had never met anyone who had ever been to Luxembourg. I went into a couple of pubs, but the place was so quiet, I went back to the train station and got on a train to Köln, Germany. I later found out it was Cologne, and I enjoyed a good walk around the city. Its massive cathedral was very impressive. I then caught a train to Amsterdam, Holland, via Duisburg and Dusseldorf. It was late when I arrived in Amsterdam. After walking around the red-light district and having my dinner in McDonald's, I went into the train station, as it was now late at night and the next train wasn't until early next morning, going to Rotterdam. I slept on a wooden bench outside the train station. I was later told that was a dangerous thing to do, as people said there were gangs of Africans running about who would stab you and mug you, but no one bothered me.

In the morning I got a train to Rotterdam. I really liked it with all its trams bombing about and tall buildings. I had a great day there, and I even stayed in a small hotel that night as a treat to myself. The next day I got a train to Brussels and then back to Ostend, then the boat home. On the boat back, I noticed a small group of men at a table playing cards, with a lot of money on the table. I thought they were probably lorry drivers, then one of them popped his head up, and I recognised him as an old villain from London, who I knew very well. He said, "Alright, Rog. I can't talk right now as I'm a bit busy." I just nodded and walked away laughing. I got home after four days of seeing Belgium, Luxembourg, Germany, and Holland, mostly just train stations, but at least I had been to those locations. Then I was back to work on the Tuesday, and the bricklayers would say to me, "What did you do for the weekend, then?" They all thought I was mad.

One year later, a few of my old schoolmates were going to Spain for two weeks and someone had pulled out, so they asked me if I'd like to join them. Off we went from Luton Airport to Alicante, on my first-ever aeroplane, for two weeks in the sun. Whilst there, after a few days we met these two Irish girls. One of them I really fancied. We went out with them on a couple of nights, and me and her got on very well, as my brother in-law Kevin was also from Ireland, as well as my father. We only had a few days with them as they then had to go home, as our first week was their second week. I wasn't sure how I felt, as I hadn't been with many girls, due to boxing all the time whilst growing up, but I thought I may have been in love.

The second week dragged on a bit as most of my mates had spent all their money and were skint. The holiday rep in our hotel said there was a big bullfight in the old town that night, but you couldn't get tickets for it as it was the most famous bullfighter, El Cordobes, doing a return one-off bullfight, as he had been retired. I thought I'd like to see that, and being from London I wasn't going to be put off by a travel rep. I caught a bus to the old town and the arena. I approached a couple of ticket touts, and I got a ticket for £20. It was a circular open-air arena holding about five thousand people. The main centre was all sand with small wooden walls dotted around the perimeter that looked like they had railway sleepers between two posts. I was quite excited when the first bull came out and started running about. The young trainee matadors came out and started to bait the bull. There were about six matadors, and they were getting the poor bull to run at each of them in turn. Every time the bull got close, they would jump behind the wooden walls, and after thirty minutes the bull was knackered.

Then the great El Cordobes came out to massive cheers from the Spanish crowd. He played with the bull for a while, going down on one knee as the bull flew past him. I would have to admit he was very brave. Although the bull was already tired out by the trainees, it was still a massive and heavy-looking animal. I was surprised the cloak he used wasn't bright red; it was yellow on one side and pink on the other. Two horseback riders came out with all chain mail hanging down either side of the horses for protection, and the bull ran at the horses a couple of times before El Cordobes pulled out two short swords and stuck them into the back of the bull's neck. The crowd was going wild, but I couldn't see the fascination myself.

At one point a young man from the crowd jumped over the fence into the bullring, and he sprinted across to the other side with the bull chasing him, then he jumped over the fence and back into the crowd with the crowd cheering wildly. Apparently, it was a bit of a ritual for newlyweds. The wife would push her new husband over the fence, and he had to get across the bullring to the other side to show how macho he was. The bullfights continued for about another three or four bulls, and I was getting bored with it all now. I felt sorry for the bulls, who didn't stand a chance and were just being played with, then killed. If they have a good performance, the bullfighter is rewarded by cutting one ear off the bull as a trophy. If it's really very good and the crowd keeps applauding, they are allowed to cut both the bull's ears off, and if it is an extremely brilliant performance, the crowd will continue to applaud and the bullfighter can then also cut the bull's tail off, all to keep as a reward. The last bull I saw El Cordobes play with, he got to cut the ears off and the tail. I found out later this was a very rare occurrence.

We were only a day before returning home from Benidorm when we met these two blokes similar in age to us, both called Pete, from Essex. They were a good laugh and bumming around Benidorm with no thought for where their lives would take them. They had no place to stay, and they just slept wherever they could, shacking up with girls and lads like us or anyone who would let them sleep on their hotel floor. We were in this open-air disco by a pool, which was fairly crowded with holidaymakers from all over, dancing and having a good time. There were these two beautiful Dutch girls swinging in these hanging wicker chairs like the one in the *Emmanuelle* films.

One of these Petes tried to chat one up, but she told him where to go. He picked up a ketchup squeezy bottle from a table and squirted the ketchup all over the back of her swinging chair. It went through all the gaps and onto the back of her dress, and she jumped off swearing and they ran away with the two Petes laughing. I just thought it was stupid myself. Moments later they came back with two enormous Dutch blokes, both about six feet four, who were very angry and aggressive. One of them started shoving one of the Petes. The other Pete picked up a bottle. I got between them to try to calm things down. When this Dutch bloke put his back in front of me and said, "Piss off, arsehole." I spun him around by reaching up to his shoulder, and then I jumped in the air and hit him with one of the best right-handed punches I think I have ever thrown. He went down like the tallest tree in the forest just felled. The two Petes set about the other one by smashing bottles into him from every angle. We had to leg it then before the police came. I jumped over this one-metre-high wall, not realising it was two metres on the other side. I hit the floor twisting my ankle, but I managed to hobble back to the hotel. I never saw the two Petes ever again, and we flew home the next morning.

I finished my bricklaying apprenticeship on 4 July 1980. I was now officially a time-served bricklayer. That summer I bought a ticket to go to Lisbon, Portugal, via a train journey from Paris. I set off, looking forward to seeing Portugal, but when I got off the train in Paris, I had about one hour to get across Paris to Montparnasse Station and my train on to Lisbon. I went down the stairs to the Metro underground. It was about 8:00 a.m. and rush hour, but most people were coming out and up the stairs whilst I was trying to go down. I asked this man if he spoke Anglaise and what was going on. He replied, "It is the Metro. They go on strike." I came out on to the main street and the queue for taxis went around the block. I really didn't know what to do. I wandered back into the train station and saw the train I had just got off was going back, so I hopped on it and went back to London.

When I arrived home, my mother was shocked and said, "You're supposed to be in Portugal." I then explained what had happened. I now had two weeks with nothing to do. After getting back from Spain, I had been swapping letters with the Irish girl, but I had stopped writing a few months earlier as I couldn't see it going anywhere. I decided out of the blue to write to her to see what she was doing. I got a reply a couple of days later, and after another day I decided to go over to Ireland to see her. Everyone thought I was mad as the Troubles were still bad over there in 1980, but I had no fear being a Londoner with an Irish father and him a former tunnel man.

I had a good week there, and everyone treated me well. There were lots of British soldiers and UDR men, along with the usual RUC police all over the place, but none of them bothered me. Her whole family were nice to me, and I enjoyed meeting them all. The only scary times were when I had walked her home late at night and I would then have to walk through the very republican council estate back to the hotel in the centre where I was staying. I went back to London thinking I was madly in love. We kept writing, and she came over to London for a weekend in October. We decided she would move over to London and we'd get a flat together.

Back at John Laing's, I got summoned to the head office in Mill Hill to see the London regional director. He said they had been very impressed with my attitude throughout my three-year apprenticeship, and they would like me to stay with them and become the youngest-ever John Laing site manager. "You'll have your own site by the age of twenty," he said confidently. I told him I wanted to see what the industry was like as a whole, and to work for various other companies to get more experience, then I could come back to John Laing's as a much better and more experienced man. He wasn't very happy.

I left John Laing's and became a self-employed bricklayer. Over the three years of my apprenticeship, 1977 to 1980, I had gone from sixteen to nineteen years old, and I wasn't really into drinking beer, due to my boxing. A schoolmate of ours that I used to go to Spurs with had got engaged to his girlfriend just after leaving school, and a couple of months later they were getting married. We all went out for his stag night to a nightclub in central London. It was good fun until some of our other mad Spurs mates turned up unexpectedly. From there being about ten of us, we were now in a group of about twenty-five. There were some blokes there I did not know. We left the club about 2:00 a.m. and walked or staggered down the Strand past Charing Cross Station past some shops, and we came across a burger place.

We all piled in to get something to eat, but the men behind the counter came out and said they were closed, as they were mopping the floor and cleaning behind the counter. Some of them had no shirts on and were sweating. In between the seats they had imitation plants and trees. Some of these Spurs fans who I did not know started to pull these plants and trees out and were throwing them at each other. These big Greek blokes – we call them Bubbles, as rhyming slang for *Greek* is *bubble and squeak* – came running towards us throwing punches, and two of them had machetes. I thought, *this is getting serious.*

A mate of mine ran up the road to Charing Cross Station, and outside the station were granite stone planters – each stone was about 100mm square. He broke a few off and came back and stood beside me in the middle of the road outside the burger bar. The commotion had all spilt out onto the pavement and road now. I saw another mate kick the window of a shoe shop next door, and the glass pane fell out onto the pavement. Another lad was trying to smash an electrical shop window on the other side of the burger bar. Two of these Bubbles came running at me and my mate, so he threw the granite stones at them, hitting them both on the head, and they fell over out cold onto the pavement. Next thing I knew, I was being dragged by a policeman who had me around the neck, and he bundled me into the back of a police van. We were all taken to the local police station, fingerprinted, and put in cells – four to a cell in three different cells, twelve of us in all.

The Spurs blokes that I did not know and who started it all were not caught and had legged it. This Spurs mate of mine in my cell kept kicking the door shouting for a cigarette and calling the police pigs. Someone came and started unlocking the door. I thought they were coming to give him a cigarette. I was the closest to the door, and I got a punch in the mouth from the policeman who had opened the door. "Shut up!" he shouted. I spat a small bit of tooth out, looked at him, and said, "Is that the best you can do?" He just scurried away. We were kept in overnight and marched into the dock of the court the next morning, all twelve of us. The magistrate fined each one £50 for threatening behaviour, working his way along the line until he got to me and my mate at the end. "And finally, you two were the ringleaders, and have been charged with causing an affray, criminal damage to property and grievous bodily harm. You will be bailed to reappear here at a later date. I suggest you get legal representation before then." We were led out of the dock and outside onto the pavement still hungover, and most of the lads were laughing it all off, but I knew me and my mate were being used as scapegoats and we were in some serious trouble.

I told my parents all about it, and I explained we were being used as scapegoats by the police, as it was convenient for them. My father was good about it, and he said, "These things happen." He knew a good solicitor who would get me a good QC barrister. This friend of my father's got me a good QC, and it would cost me £50 cash every time he appeared on my behalf at the magistrate court. I was only earning £19 a week, but I had about £200 saved that I would have to use. The two of us appeared at the court another three times over the next eight months, as the police kept asking for adjournments, which was very frustrating and costing me £50 a time. The QC was only in court for about ten minutes every time and for £50! It all eventually concluded. We were in court No. 1 at the top of the stairs for the whole day, only breaking for lunch for an hour. That QC really earnt his money on the last day, as he was in court the whole day and tore the opposition apart, including all the Greek witnesses. He was superb. It all got settled, and we were dismissed with all charges dropped. What a result.

I should have learnt my lesson then and stayed away from bad influences, but I'm sure some of my friends could say the same about me, as I did enjoy a good fight. My wise old boxing trainer Tony said to me, after he had appeared in court for me as a character witness, "It can't always be someone else's fault, Roger. Eventually people will think it's you."

I carried on meeting up with old schoolmates at a notorious old pub. After finishing at college on my evening class I'd go to the pub to meet up with friends, and on a Saturday night I usually ventured up there or to the local working men's club, as we knew most of the people drinking there. The pub was full of villains and lunatics. The older villains and armed robbers were known as the A-Team, and the younger ones like us were known as the B-Team.

There was always trouble in the pub, especially when there was a big sporting event on at Wembley, as the pub had a large car park at the front, which was ideal for coaches. The police would quite often raid the pub and remove various weapons hidden in the toilet cisterns of the gent's and ladies' toilets – knives, hatchets, cleavers, etc.

A couple of friends of ours were inseparable, and one of their brothers had just been released from a long stretch inside – prison, that is – and the brother, who knew no other way of life, talked the two of them into helping him get some quick cash. He stole a car and put it in a lock-up garage until he was ready to do the robbery with it. What he didn't realise was the Sweeney, the police section that targeted notorious armed robbers. *Sweeney Todd* was cockney rhyming slang for 'robbery squad' – had been watching him, as they knew he could not go straight and would rob again.

When the day of the robbery arrived a week later, they were going to do a London sub post office. One of our mates sat in the car whilst the two brothers entered the post office with sawn-off shotguns. The car door was pulled open, and the driver had a gun put to his head. The police officer said, "Don't fucking move." He naturally froze to the seat. When the two robbers came out, they were confronted by the police running across the road towards them. They ran down the side road, and my mate slung the shotgun into a garden. They caught up with him and pinned him to the ground with a gun at his head, and he said, "Fuck me, this wasn't in the script!" I always laugh when I recall those words.

When it was all over, our mate who threw the gun was in Maidstone, his brother was in Belmarsh, and our mate who had been the driver was in HMP Parkhurst on the Isle of Wight. A mate of mine visited him in HMP Parkhurst, and he told me it was very scary on the Isle of Wight visiting Parkhurst. They had the biggest screws in all the UK prisons, and my mate was six feet tall and looked like a dwarf near these blokes. My visiting mate had been given instructions to bring with him some weed, wrapped in clingfilm. When my mate took a seat in the visitor's hall, the inmates walked in and sat opposite each of their visitors. Our inmate friend said, "Did you bring the gear?" The visitor nodded. "Pass it under the table nice and slowly," he said, but with the nerves the man dropped it and it rolled out into the centre of the aisle. There was a massive screw standing at the end of each aisle with their peaked caps almost down to their noses. Luckily this one hadn't noticed, so the visitor got up and picked it up quickly and passed it to our inmate friend, who quickly stuck it up his arse as he had cut his overalls to allow this to be done. My friend told me afterwards he was thinking all the way home that he could have got banged up if caught supplying an inmate, and he liked his freedom.

Quite often from our pub we'd go up to a large Irish-type dance club in North London, but not to have fun and pull a girl. It was just to fight with the bouncers. The A-Team could not get in as they were too well known, but some of us B-Team could grab a girl, tell her we were paying for her, and get in as a couple, then tell the girl to piss off once we were in and conveniently behind the bouncers.

The A-Team would attack them from across the road from the front, and we would fly into them from the back. On a couple of occasions, we would walk away, leaving the bouncers lying on the pavement. It all stopped when one of the older blokes went too far and decided to shoot a bouncer. I remember him being in the pub on the Saturday night with a brown canvas bag. A mate of mine sat down beside me and said, "He's got a gun in the bag to do one of the bouncers." The sad thing was he shot the wrong bouncer. It made me feel sick when I heard what had happened, as even though I was usually on the wrong side of the law, I was still aware of the basics of what was right and wrong, and this was very wrong.

Another lad in our pub was always nicking cars, then looking for a police car to chase him, but one night it all went wrong, and he had a head-on collision. He survived but spent a long time in hospital and had a metal plate inserted into his head. A year or so later he was dead, killed by another mate from the pub. He had been two-timing this fella's sister, and the fella wasn't happy. He came into the pub with a baseball bat looking for my mate. Someone told him he had gone over to the local club. This fella went out, and the barman called the club to warn my mate that this bloke was coming over to do him. My mate left the club and walked back towards the pub. They met in the subway under the main road, and he was battered to death by the nutter with the baseball bat. I don't think he realised he had a metal plate in his head, which meant he got a lighter sentence when in court.

In the same year, we had a second killing attached to the pub. I refrain from using any real names, as it would not be fair to relatives and friends still alive today. We had a little firm that would go to see Tottenham Hotspur FC – the Spurs – play football at White Hart Lane. Our leader, who I will call Ted, was a lunatic from the top drawer and completely fearless. At a Spurs v. Man United football match, we were fighting down Seven Sisters Road, and me and Ted got separated from the others.

Ted pointed to this United supporter wearing a nice sheepskin coat and said, "I want that coat." We ran towards the man, and Ted pulled out a knife and stuck it straight into the man's stomach.

He took the coat off him and slung it to me to catch: "Hold that while I get him out into the road."

I shouted, "What are you doing?" as I could hear sirens everywhere and there was a big red bus coming down the road towards us.

"The bus will run over him, and they won't know he's been stabbed."

I dropped the coat and ran. After the Spurs matches, we would meet up in a local pub near Kings Cross Station. I walked into the pub, and the others were already there and said, "Where did you and Ted go?" I explained what had happened. Then Ted walked in with the sheepskin coat on.

We were at Spurs v. Newcastle for a midweek league cup replay, and in those days at White Hart Lane, they would give the whole Park Lane terraced end to the away supporters if there were enough of them. This night there must have been ten thousand Geordies in the Park Lane end. We were from the Paxton Road end, where most of the old-school hard Spurs men were based. They had metal gates to the terraces in the four corners of the ground then, and on this night the gates were all open. That meant you could walk around the whole perimeter of terraces, apart from the all-seated West Stand. Ted said, "Come on, let's spice things up a bit." We all followed him around the ground to the Park Lane end.

We worked our way through the Geordie fans to behind the goal, then Ted just started hitting as many Geordies as possible, and we all followed suit. All I remember was punches raining down on me from everywhere. I was relieved when the police moved in and pulled us out of there. They evicted us from the ground. None of us were too badly beat up, just bruises mostly. Ted knew the man on the gate at Paxton Road, who let us back in. Ted stood up onto a metal terrace rail with us holding his legs so he didn't fall off of it, and he took his shirt off, twirling it around his head, baiting the Geordies. We were all singing, "Tottenham aggro, Tottenham aggro."

I remember when we beat Chelsea to relegate them to division 2 in 1978/79. We were fighting on the pitch and just hitting anyone near us. I'm sure we hit some of our own supporters – it was all very stupid.

Ted was working on a roof of a house a few yards away from a pub. A man he had been looking for from an earlier falling-out somewhere walked past the house and along the road and entered the car park of the pub. Ted had gone down the ladder and caught up with him in the pub car park. Words were said, Ted hit him several times, knocking him to the floor, and Ted went on to give him a severe beating. The victim's best mate, who happened to be a lunatic from another pub nearby, heard what had happened and was not happy with Ted. Ted was told about this but just said, "Fuck him."

A couple of weeks later, I was in the pub sitting chatting to someone at a table. Ted was at the bar with another friend when this irate mate of the victim walked into the pub. The friend at the bar said to Ted, "Here comes that irate mate." Once again Ted put his pint to his mouth and said, "Fuck him." Then *whoosh*! A knife was plunged straight into Ted's neck from the side. He hit the floor, and I jumped up. The mate at the bar tried to stop the blood, and they managed to carry him out to a car to get him to the nearest hospital, but he was dead when they got there.

Later at the court hearing, many of the lads from the pub testified in the killer's favour, so that he would get a lighter sentence and they could then kill him when he was released from prison. That's how mad it all was then at that pub. The police made the brewery change the pub name, trying to take away its notoriety and violent history, but it didn't work, and you still had many lunatics drinking and fighting there for a number of years until it was finally demolished.

Being a boxer meant I was never really one of the madder ones in the pub. Using weapons or tools was not my thing then at that age. I just had good punches that I always found quite adequate in dispatching opponents. I did get a bit of a reputation for fighting whilst driving – road rage. There were many occasions when I'd find myself up before the magistrate courts for GBH or ABH (grievous bodily harm or actual bodily harm), usually getting bound over to keep the peace for twelve months or a suspended sentence for twelve months. I just didn't like people I saw as bullies, when they cut me up or drove stupidly around me.

One funny incident whilst I was driving to work in the early morning: this idiot with his girlfriend cut right in front of me, then found that he had to jam the anchors on as the traffic light had turned red. I braked hard and swerved so as not to hit his car. I jumped out and he got out, too. I smashed him with a good right punch that would knock out most men, but this large soft lump with a thick neck just looked rather put out. He was probably a second-row rugby player for some posh team. Luckily there was the old faithful left hook following close behind. As that struck across the target, his jaw, he went down like a sack of shit. I hadn't realised his girlfriend had come up behind me and jumped on me, wrapping her legs around me from behind and digging her fingernails into my neck. I bent down and threw her over my shoulder. She landed on the grass in the middle of the road with her skirt up around her neck, showing off some very nice black stockings and suspenders with nice white panties. I would have loved to stay and admire the view, but I jumped into my car and was off like a shot.

On another occasion we were on our way home from a site and driving through NW London. Me driving with two mates in the car. I pulled up slowly behind this blond lady in her car in front of me. As I came to a stop in the stationary traffic, this big bloke got out of his van and walked back to this car sitting in front of us and started to give it the big-un to the blond lady sitting petrified and gripping her steering wheel. I got out and had a go at this bloke to leave her alone. He turned to me and said, "Oh, you want some tough guy," and he came at me like a steam train. I managed to sway my head back and crouch a little to avoid the first two punches he threw, then I came back with a couple of nice combinations, and I finished it off by bashing his head several times onto this lady's car wing. I remember her shocked face with her mouth wide open. She was probably worried about her car getting dented. Leaving him in the road, we all drove away and around his van. I said to my two mates in my car, "Isn't it funny how they are the toughest men in the world before you hit them?"

Most of the road rage incidents happened early in the morning, and usually on my way to work. I am not a morning person. Another occasion we were driving to work at about 6:30 a.m. when this Jamaican couple were crossing the road but taking forever and moving very slowly. I sounded my car horn and they started shouting at me, with the man getting very aggressive. I got out and confronted him, and he hit me, just scraping the side of my face. I gave him a few good whacks, and he had his head down near my waist, but he was as strong as an ox and he now had his hands digging into my neck scratching me. I finished him off with another couple of punches, and he dropped to his knees. His wife came at me from the side, and she hit me with her handbag. The purse fell out and I kicked it, spilling loads of coins all over the place, making me laugh. I ran back to the car, and I sped away. My mates in the car were just laughing, and when we arrived at the site to start work at 7:30 a.m., they took great delight in telling the foreman what had happened. I walked in after being in the toilets washing the deep scratches in my neck that were quite painful. The foreman just looked at me and shook his head.

One time I was driving to a job in Hounslow. I went along a country road with low hedges on either side. I was in my old escort van full of builder's tools and dust and dirt. It was about 6:30 a.m. and quiet, when this car came speeding up behind me from nowhere with two young blokes in it. They started to toot their horn, and I noticed in my rear-view mirror they were doing the wanker sign at me, and then they sped past, nearly knocking me into the hedge at the side of the road. As they went past, the passenger was hanging out the window doing the wanker gestures to me. It would be fair to say they had picked on the wrong bloke. I accelerated as fast as I could, and I rammed the rear of their car full on. My van filled up with dust in the air so I couldn't see anything, and my front windscreen cracked right up the middle. The vehicles were locked together but still moving, I braked, and my van came free from their rear bumper. I then drove around to alongside them, and I rammed the passenger front corner of my van into the driver's door. The driver's face was a picture.

They went off the road and into the hedges. I nearly hit a car coming towards me on the wrong side of the road, so I quickly swerved back in on to the right side of the road. As I sped away, I looked in my rear-view mirror, and I could see their car going through the hedges and into the field and out of sight. I got to work, and my work mates said, "What happened to your van?" I explained what had happened, and they just all burst out laughing. It was fortunate I hadn't stopped to beat those blokes up, as it was now just a motoring offence of leaving the scene of an accident without swapping particulars and not a criminal violent offence.

When I went to court, I was ordered to pay £500 compensation to them, and I got six points on to my license. It was sometime later that a magistrate in Willesden magistrates court made me see sense, when he said to me in the dock, "You cannot put the world to rights, Roger. Let someone else do that, and you can stay out of court." I came away thinking, *He's right. There are bullies and idiotic drivers everywhere – I'll be fighting every day of the week.* I calmed down a lot after that, but every now and then the demons would surface.

I was lying in bed one Saturday night in our tower block flat when I heard a lot of shouting and arguing below in the small open-air shopping centre that was at the bottom and rear of our flats. I looked out of my window, and I could see the empty first-floor outdoor car park below and the spiral metal stairs in the centre that provided drivers with access to the shops below. There was a pub on the ground floor beside the stairs and an alleyway, and it had a nightclub attached to it. The raised voices continued, and I could see several people around the bottom and up a bit on the spiral stairs. Then I heard a woman screaming, followed by the sickly sound of a man screaming. That is not a nice sound to hear. I shut the window and went back to sleep.

In the morning, I looked out and I could see policemen all over the place searching. I found out a young pot man working in the nightclub had told the bouncers to evict a couple of blokes he didn't like. They came back at the end of the night and waited for him to leave the club. They – three men and a girl – set upon him with two knives and cut him to pieces, killing him. The police eventually caught the killers; two came from my flats. I knew them but only to say hello to. The other two were from the block of flats next to mine. This seemed to be a bad time for my area.

Across on the other side of the green there was a nice small shoe shop. I got to know the Italian man who owned it quite well, as I loved Italian moccasin shoes. Whenever I walked near the shop, he would sometimes be outside the shop and have a chat with me, as he loved boxing. I went across the green one Sunday, and there was a policeman standing outside the shop, and there was police blue-and-white tape across the shop door. I asked what had happened, but the policeman just told me to move along. I found out the following week in the local paper that the owner had been shot dead. He regularly held a game of poker above the shop after they closed on a Saturday night, and one of the players must have lost heavily or had a row with the other players. The shop then closed permanently.

One of the benefits of living in West London was the BBC were all around us. We had the BBC Theatre that hosted Bruce Forsyth's *Generation Game*, *The Two Ronnies*, *Steptoe and Son*, *Crackerjack!*, Dave Allen, and my favourite, *The Old Grey Whistle Test*. They were all free to get in, and I got to know the man on the door, old Stan. I could walk there to see *The Old Grey Whistle Test* and sit down to watch all the different music acts live as it was being filmed. There were cables all over the stage floor, and these massive TV cameras filming. I would always go upstairs and watch from the small balcony. A man would come out and tell us all to follow the signs that he would hold up. Then whispering Bob Harris would walk out, and this man would hold up a sign with *CLAP* on it in large letters – how very basic.

One of the best acts I saw was an hour special with Jackson Browne in 1976. He had the album of the year, *The Pretender*, and he wrote *Take It Easy* for the Eagles. He stood at a microphone and played a guitar, then he sat at a piano. What a very talented man, and a great songwriter. In my last year at school and the next years of my teens I saw many live bands at various concert venues, like the Eagles' Hotel California tour at Wembley Empire Pool; Fleetwood Mac's Rumours tour at Finsbury Park Rainbow Theatre; Steve Miller Band; Jonathan Richman and the Modern Lovers at Hammersmith Odeon; and one concert I will always remember, Lynyrd Skynyrd at Hammersmith Odeon. I did not know who they were, a friend just said, "Roger, I have a spare ticket. Would you like to come as you live just up the road from Hammersmith?" I must say most of the concert was very boring for me, but they finished with *Sweet Home Alabama* which I thought was good. They had a massive Confederate flag across the back of the stage. They went off and we were cheering as you do, and they came back on and did their encore, *Free Bird*.

I had never heard anything like it. It was amazing, and the lead guitarist built it up until near the end in a frenzy he came out on the long, extended piece of the stage and lay on his back. He was dressed all in white, and the spotlight went on him in the dark. With just this white circle of light on him playing the guitar on his back on the floor. If you know the song, you can imagine what it was like –

incredible. I was very fortunate to see them, as later that year they were in a plane crash and several of them died.

One band I did miss out on and silly me turned down a ticket – I have regretted that ever since – was Led Zeppelin live at Earl's Court, although a mate of mine went and said, "They were so far away you could hardly see them."

I was going out with this girl from the local girls' convent school, and she really liked the soul group called the Stylistics. I came home from school one day, and my mother said the lady from the flat upstairs, who worked in the Royal Albert Hall box office, had dropped in two tickets for a music concert, and she thought you might like them. I looked at the tickets, and they were for the Stylistics next week. What about that for a bit of luck. We went to the concert, which was not really my type of music, but they were very good singers all dressed in red velvet suits, standing in a row and dancing in time to every song. There was no stopping; they just went from one song to another without stopping. The whole concert was over in under an hour. When we came out, people were queueing to go in for the next concert. They were doing three concerts a night. Anyway, my girlfriend was very happy, and that was all that mattered. Jonathan Richman and the Modern Lovers were very funny. They had hit singles with *Egyptian Reggae* and *Roadrunner* in the charts here but weren't very well known. Most groups would have a support band on first, but they had a juggler, which was different and very entertaining. At the end they came back on for an encore, and they sang their song, *Ice Cream Man* which goes on a bit at the end. They left the stage and we got up to leave, then they came back on again and went back into *Ice Cream Man* we all sat down again. This happened three more times, then we, along with everyone else, just kept walking out of the arena, but they were still on the stage singing *Ice Cream Man* for the fifth time and laughing themselves silly. Talk about being different, they were unique and very funny musicians.

Chapter Six
Leaving Home

In October 1980, my girlfriend came over to London and we moved into a rented house in West London. We shared it with another young couple, and it was £40 per week to rent. It wasn't long before she got a job and we got engaged to be married.

It's worth pointing out at this stage that I was still a virgin. I had misspent my whole youth boxing, and any girlfriends I had seemed to just want me to escort them everywhere like a trophy bloke, to look after them. We did all the petting and foreplay, but I never really got past first base with most of them. I expect talking about boxing all the time wasn't very sexy. After a couple of months, an old friend of my boxing trainer who was a landlord and owned a few properties around West London offered us a flat of our own on the top floor of a large house near Paddington, just a hundred yards from the tube station, for just £20 per week. We were very happy there, and we went back to Ireland to be married in a big Catholic church.

One year later, and our son James was born in Hammersmith Hospital, East Acton, next door to Wormwood Scrubs Prison. As she was in labour for the whole night, I remember looking out at the prison windows next door. Some windows had their lights on all night, and I thought about two friends of mine who would be in there for another five years. It was a difficult birth, and there were complications after the baby was born. There was a tear in her womb that wouldn't stop bleeding internally, so she was rushed off for an emergency operation. It was a funny feeling, as I'd spent nine months worrying if the baby would be born okay with no defects, but I never worried about my wife, and here I was with a beautiful baby son, but my wife was at death's door. I was twenty-one years old, and I was now watching a Catholic priest give her the last rites. My father came and sat with me while they operated on her. It all turned out well, and we moved back in with my parents into their flat, to give us some time to save for our own place.

I was working on large building sites all over London, and being a tough man who had an excellent bricklaying schooling, I became a foreman bricklayer, supervising the brickwork element of the buildings. It wasn't easy being so young and in charge of much older tradesmen. I was on one site in Wandsworth, South London, where the bricklayers gave me a hard time. I sacked a few of them and I had to knock one of them out to get a bit of respect. The job didn't go very well, and I think the subby was losing money. He turned up one day in his big Merc, and he had another bloke with him. He introduced him and said this man was his best foreman and he had just become free. I was going to be the No. 2 starting the next day. I got all cocky and said, "Well you can stick your job. I'm not a No. 2 for anyone," and I walked off.

I had earnt quite a bit of money, and we had enough for a deposit on a ground-floor two-bed flat with our own garden just outside West London that cost £21,500 with a lease for ninety-nine years. I went to a building society to see the manager about a mortgage for £20,000. As I was self-employed, he wanted to see three years of accounts, but I only had one year, so I copied the one year I had from my accountant, and I then changed some of the figures to make up another two years of accounts. When I gave them to the manager, he looked through them, and to my relief he handed them back to me and said, "They are fine," and he gave me the mortgage.

The flat needed lots of work, but it was mostly just bits of plastering and tiling and modernising the sinks and bath. I also built a nice stone fireplace and a nice patio of stone slabs with small stone walls around it. We moved out of my parents' flat in late 1982 and into our own place. We were very happy with our own little family and our own place. Most of the neighbours were quite old, but all were very nice. There was a large detached house next door to the left. The couple there were Polish, and the man had been a hero pilot during the war and stayed here after the war.

There was an RAF base just up the road, and a pilot there used to take a Spitfire plane up in the air once or twice a year. I had lived there for about six months when the Polish man next door told me to go out into the garden, as this pilot, who was a friend of his, would fly low over his garden in the next twenty minutes. We all went out into the garden, and you could see him coming in the Spitfire – then whoosh! Over he came, and the plane was only a few hundred feet above us, and he was tilting the plane sideways. You could see all of the underside and the noise was deafening, but what a sight! It made the hairs on the back of my neck stand up. What a fantastic aeroplane. It won us the war, and all those brave young pilots not knowing if each mission could be their last. It was a real treat to get to see the plane so close flying by, and I thanked our neighbour, who had tears in his eyes.

Around this time my wife had several check-ups at hospital, and we were told it would be dangerous for her to get pregnant again in the next five years. We had a discussion and decided it would also not be good for her to be on the pill for the next five years, either. I spoke to the doctor and asked him about a vasectomy. He said he knew a good clean surgeon who could do it, but as I was only twenty-two years old it would have to be done privately. I was given an appointment, and I met this nice old surgeon with white hair. He mentioned how young I was and what if my wife and I got divorced at some time in the future. That just sounded ridiculous to me at that time – I just couldn't see it happening. He explained that the operation could be reversed but not with any guaranteed success. I signed a form for him to proceed with the operation, which would cost £150.

I had the operation some weeks later at the local hospital, and I returned to work laying bricks afterwards, but I only lasted about an hour as the anaesthetic had worn off, then I went home to bed. Before the operation, the surgeon was talking to me about my building work, and he said he had a large house in Buckinghamshire that needed the chimneys repointed. He gave me his address and said, "Maybe when the weather gets better in a couple of months, you could pop by and have a look at the chimneys for me." I replied, "Yes of course I will."

My mate and I kept doing small jobs here and there for various people. One day a job fell through, as they were not ready for us when we turned up. I had not told my mate about my vasectomy, as I was a bit embarrassed about it and I thought it a private matter. I suddenly remembered the old surgeon and his chimneys. I drove my mate into Buckinghamshire, telling him I may have a job for us. We arrived at what I would describe as a mansion, set in a few acres of prime land in a very expensive area.

It had been three months since my operation, and I wasn't sure if the surgeon would be in, or if he would remember me, but we had nothing else on, so it was worth a shot. I knocked on the large oak door with my mate standing right behind me. The surgeon answered the door and said, "Ah, Mr Byrne, and how's your genitals?"

I froze momentarily, then said, "They're fine thank you."

I looked at my mate, who looked like he had seen a ghost.

I said, "I'll explain later."

We fell about laughing later when I explained it all to him, and I've had many laughs with that one over the years since then. We went on to point the chimneys, and he paid us very good money. What a gent!

We had some funny mates who did labouring for us at times, what you would call proper hod-carriers and proper old-school. We were building the foundations for a couple of houses, and one of the men said to me, "I'll load out the bricks for you on Saturday morning for a price of £7 per 1,000."

I said, "Okay, that's a deal."

When I came in on Monday morning, I got the shock of my life. There were about 5,000 bricks all stacked out. Some of the stacks had fallen over into the trenches, and there were scaffold boards bridging across them, what you might call running boards. I paid him the £35 – he had earnt it. Another hoddy who used to work with us was called Bob, and he told us he had just got a new tattoo on his calf. He pulled up his trouser leg to show us, and it was just ink writing. It said, *Bob's Leg*.

We said, "That's mad."

Then he said, "Wait to see this," and he lifted his trouser up on the opposite leg, and there was another tattoo that read, *Bob's Other Leg*.

We just fell about laughing – what great characters on the sites. The next three years were mostly uneventful. I was boxing now and again, with my wife staying at home all the time looking after our son, who was doing well and walking and talking now. We went back to Ireland quite often to see her family.

In 1983 I applied for a job as an assistant site manager through an agency, and they sent me for an interview to a site in Victoria, just a stone's throw away from Buckingham Palace. It was the largest refurbishment project in London, at £50 million, that involved the St James Hotel, a very old and iconic building with very old ornamental craftsmanship to the brickwork and ornate plaster work to the rooms inside. I was pleased when I arrived to see the main contractor was John Laing's. This director of the management contractor that had subbed the work from John Laing's interviewed me and seemed impressed with my passion for my trade and the historic workmanship around us. He said, "Let's go for a walk around the site."

As we did, every John Laing manager who passed us said, "Hello, Roger, how have you been?"

He was very impressed, and the main John Laing manager told him to employ me, that I'd do just fine on the project. They offered me the job, and I phoned my father to ask his advice, to see if I should go for it or not. His reply to me was, "They can't cut your arms and legs off, can they? The worst they can do to you is sack you."

I turned up on the following Monday, a twenty-two-year-old assistant site manager and ready to conquer the world. My boss was the main site manager, and he was about forty years of age. I introduced myself. He said he had heard lots of good things about me, and if I was ready to listen, he would teach me as much as he could, which I thought was very decent of him. It was a difficult job, and I had to stay on at night until about 8:00 p.m. just to get my paperwork done. It was hard work, especially looking after welders, demolition labourers, carpenters, bricklayers, and bricklayers' labourers. Some of them were giving me the run around, but I was street wise enough to stand up to the cocky ones, and I sacked a couple.

One of the big elements of the work was cutting down the old fire escape stairways on the outside of the building going up about six floors; that was a lot of scrap going into lorries. After my first week, I turned up on the following Monday and was changing in my office into my site gear when the director who had interviewed me came in and sat down. He then explained to me they'd had to sack the main site manager, as he was stealing lorries of scrap and directing them to his mate who owned a scrapyard in East London. I was shocked. He then said he was going to be based permanently on site from now on and I was to run the project, with a hefty wage increase. I said okay, but it was too much for me really. I was getting pulled all over the place, and I had to attend several meetings a week with Laing's senior management. This went on for about three weeks.

The director had not been on site for three days when a senior Laing manager called me into his office. He told me the company had gone bust, and I was to round up my men in the centre square of the hotel and tell them the bad news. I went outside, shocked and a bit confused. I had never been in this position before, and now I had to tell over a hundred men that they were out of work and had lost two weeks wages as well. This was at 8:30 a.m. in the morning. As I looked at the crowd of faces in front of me, it was very sad, as I had got to know most of them, and I told them the bad news.

They understandably went mad, and one gang of tough guys wanted to lynch me as I was the only manager there. I explained to them that I had lost two weeks' money as well, and I was just as pissed off as they were. A couple of them pushed me but luckily, I had helped out an old armed robber mate from White City who had just got out of prison after a ten-year stretch. I'd given him work knocking down walls on the site with a couple of his pals, and they were very happy and grateful to me for that. He stepped in and said, "No one touches Rog; it's not his fault." They all backed away very quickly.

The men barricaded the site entrances with skips. They stole every bit of plant from our stores, like Hilti guns, drills, heavy-duty Kango breakers, and anything they thought they could sell. John Laing's called the police, and as Scotland Yard and Buckingham Palace were only around the corner they came very quickly. There were a few scuffles, then the union reps turned up to make the demonstration more official, and the police backed off. I went to a meeting with John Laing's managers and the union official. John Laing's had paid the company in advance, just a week earlier, to help them out and to allow them to continue, but when they banked the cheque, the bank froze their account and put them under. All the union man could do was to tell the men to go to their nearest social security office and they would be given an emergency payment of about £80. That was not good as these men had been earning about £200 to £300 a week. John Laing's immediately offered me a position as an assistant site manager to stay on site, but the money was ridiculous compared to what I had been earning, and I could get more as a bricklayer. I walked away from all the chaos and madness, and the following week I was on a site laying bricks and as happy as I could be.

We sold the flat in 1985 and bought an end-of-terrace bay-fronted house. I was now a supervisor for a large brickwork contractor and earning decent money. I was a section foreman on a large site beside Tower Bridge in St Katharine Docks. It was the second phase of the original World Trade Centre, and it was called Commodity Quay. This was a very difficult project and a very prestigious one, with sixteen arches, each with a fifty-feet span. They were the largest arches in London apart from the one at St Pancras train station. I was responsible for the large arches and the piers. There was an older foreman in overall charge, and he also had another two foremen for different sections. I learnt so much from them all; they were the best traditional tradesmen and very similar to the ones who taught me whilst I was with John Laing's. The project went well, and I am very proud of the arches. Many years later I took my sons back to St Katharine Docks to see them, and there were tourists photographing them, which was nice.

The house we had just bought needed a lot of work, just like the last one had, but it didn't take me long to sort it out and update it. The following year, in 1986, I built a large extension onto it at the side and all the way across the rear of the house. I had finished the project at the World Trade Centre, Tower Bridge, and I was now building a new Sainsbury's store locally. This came in very handy as I got one of the site structural engineers to design the steel H frame I needed to carry the weight of the top floor of the house, while I knocked down the ground-floor supporting walls. I had these massive steel girders delivered, and I managed to talk a mobile crane driver we had on the site into bringing his crane around to my house after work. We blocked the whole road for about thirty minutes while we got these steel beams lowered into position, with a thousand-ton mobile crane. I went on to complete a fantastic extension to the house, transforming it into a great house to live in. The living room was about thirty feet by thirty feet, with French doors all along the rear of the house.

A friend of mine who I knew from the pub bred Staffordshire bull terrier dogs to show at dog shows. He talked me into going up to Scotland with him one weekend to get a good dog he was after, that he wanted for breeding purposes. We drove up to just north of Glasgow and came back with this dog he had wanted, and whilst there I bought a Staffordshire bull terrier puppy. We called the little staffy Jack, but my wife being Irish wanted him to be kept only in the garden and not in the house. I built a blockwork kennel for him and filled it with straw. I could lift the roof up to clean it out, and it had a passageway entrance, then a room at the back, so he could be nice and warm and away from the wind and rain. Jack got used to it, as it's all he knew. Every now and then when she was out, I'd let him come into the house just a bit. It's funny because he wasn't used to it; he'd jump straight back out into the garden.

In 1985, I started my own business. I did a couple of new houses and extensions, and I still did a few fireplaces now and again. I was doing okay, and I worked with a mate of mine. If he won a job, it was his job, and I'd work for him on wages, and similarly if I won the job, he'd work for me on wages, and it worked well. We were always busy, and our reputations were good.

One day I had a phone call from an architect I had come across on one of the large sites I had previously supervised. He had a small job in South London and asked if I could help him out, as the brickie he had there had jacked all of a sudden. He said it was only a couple of days' work for two bricklayers. Off we went the following morning in my escort van, small mixer in the back with our tools. We should have had *Have Trowel, Will Travel* on the side of my van. We arrived at the site, and a giant of an Irishman showed us what had to be done. There were two isolated brick piers, each one 450mm square, to build in the back-garden patio area to carry a roof that would come out from the main building. By lunchtime, we were both up 1.5m high, and after lunch we could put bandstand scaffolds around them and finish them by 5:00 p.m.

With it not being our local area, we looked for somewhere to have a bit of lunch and settled for this large pub near the tube station. We were having a pie and a pint and a game of pool when these six local lads came into the pub and gathered around the pool table whilst we were still playing. They put money on the edge of the table, to denote they would be playing next, but they didn't move away. It all got a bit tense, and I had to have a word with their leader. They then backed off and sat down. We finished our game and left the pub. There was no point in fighting them as they may have had at least two knives amongst them. All I had said to their leader was we did not want any trouble, but if they did, then we would accommodate them.

When we got back to the site, this big Irish foreman came up to me and started shouting that I had built the pier in the wrong bond. I told him he didn't know what he was talking about and we had built it correctly, and the only way it could be built properly as the piers were only two bricks wide. He then did an unforgiveable thing; he put his boot to my pier and pushed it over flat onto the floor. There was only one thing I could do, and I hit him with a straight right punch, but as I threw it he bent his head downwards, and I connected with his face just above his nose where it met his forehead. The skin split, and blood went down his face from his forehead. He let out a roar and picked up a four-inch square fence post and swung it at me, hitting me on the shoulder and knocking me into a shallow trench where the fencers had been digging.

I saw a straight-edged spade sitting at the side of the trench. I picked it up and I sprang to my feet. I swung the spade in a full semicircle and connected with the flat of the spade to his left ear. He went down like a ton of bricks onto the floor, and I just kept hitting him with the spade and trying to break his legs with it. My mate managed to get me to stop. We put our tools and the spade into the van and sped off. When we got back to West London, I stopped the van and threw the spade into a builder's skip at the side of the road.

That evening the architect phoned me to tell me the foreman was in hospital, and the police had my details, and the best thing I could do was go to my local police station and hand myself in. I told him I still wanted to be paid, as it was the idiot of a foreman that caused the trouble. He said no problem, and he would drop a cheque to my house tomorrow. I walked up to the police station, and I explained to the desk sergeant what had happened during the day in South London. He put me in an interview room and made some phone calls. He then told me there would be two CID men coming up to get me from South London.

They arrived about an hour later and drove me to Lambeth police station. I was interviewed and charged with GBH and looking at a stretch in prison. I did not tell my wife at the time as I didn't want to worry her, and I was always optimistic as I knew I was good in court. I had the ability to tell them what they wanted to hear, and I could speak loudly and clearly and explain about how bad I felt and how ashamed I was to be standing here before them in a court of law. The police were saying that I hit him with the spade's sharp edge, causing the cut to his forehead. I replied, "If I had hit him with a spade's sharp edge, it would probably have cut right through his head," and said there was no spade, just a good punch that caused the cut. They had no spade as evidence and no witnesses other than the victim himself.

When the time came for me to attend South West Magistrates court, I did not tell my wife, and I just went to work as normal but with a change of clothes in the van. It was funny entering the court building as it was just along the road from Battersea Town Hall, where I had experienced some great nights of boxing success. I had a good brief (QC) and was waiting to be called into the courtroom when a police officer came up and sat beside me. He asked me how I was going to plead.

I said, "Not guilty, and I shall request an old-style committal at crown court." This plea would always upset the police, as it meant several police officers would have to miss work to be cross examined by the defending brief, who would tear their evidence apart. The brief would always know when officers had compared their notes back at the station and then altered them to be exactly as each other's notes. They couldn't help themselves and fell into the trap every time. They would also not want it to go to crown court due to further cost.

These police officers then said, "We cannot prove you used a spade, so what if we drop the charge to ABH (actual bodily harm)? Would you plead guilty to that?"

I said yes, I would as no matter what, I had actually cut his head with my punch which was definitely ABH. My brief wanted me to stick to not guilty, but I wanted an end to it all and overruled him. I got a twelve months jail sentence but suspended for twelve months. What a great result.

When I got home, I told my wife, and she was not happy: "If you had gone to prison, I would be getting a phone call from you telling me you were gone for a long time. How would I have managed with our son and this house?" I think that was the beginning of the end of our marriage.

I then made yet another comeback in boxing. I had been sparring and training in a couple of different pro gyms, and I was looking good. I had passed the trainers badges as well for the boy's club so I could help with the training and be in the corner for some of the lad's bouts when out at boxing shows. My first fight back was to be at the Café Royal in Piccadilly against a lad who was the reigning Senior London ABA Champion at light-middleweight. According to my comp secretary, "Don't worry, Rog, this kid can't punch and wins all his fights on points."

It was great to be back in the ring under the lights and in front of a large audience. When the bell went to start, he came at me much quicker than I expected. This was the difference between sparring in the gyms and actually being in a proper boxing contest. He hit me many times, and my comp secretary was right. He couldn't punch, but he made up for that with his speed of punching and his movement around the ring. I couldn't get anywhere near to him. By the time we got to the third round, I thought, *I must have worn his hands out by now.* If I had been at an auction, I'd have bought everything, with my head bobbing up and down from all the punches. I lost on points and realised just how out of touch I was with the younger boxers. That was me done with boxing. I'd have to find something else to keep me fit. As the old villains used to say, "A fit body is a fit mind." I ended my official amateur boxing career with 76 bouts, 58 wins and 18 losses. I was stopped inside the distance four times, but I was never knocked out or put on the floor.

I went to my local rugby club, and I asked if I could train with them, as I had always had a fascination with rugby union ever since my father had taken me and my brother to Cardiff to watch Wales v. Ireland in the seventies. Eventually,

I got to know the first team and a few second-team players. The third, fourth and fifth teams did their own training at home or in the pub. After a month or so, the coach suggested that I turn up on the Saturday morning and get a game with the fourth or fifth teams. I thought why not, as I had only been playing on the wing in training, as I was relatively quick. I turned up and got a match, I don't know which team it was, as the fourth or fifth teams would usually be the same team, depending on how many players turned up.

Some weeks it was just the one team, and other weeks it would be both teams. The captains would hurriedly get on the phone to other rugby clubs to see if they would give both teams a game. Sometimes if a match couldn't be arranged, the fifth team would just stay at home and play a friendly match with the veterans. I played in one of those matches, and it was a good laugh, but those vets were tough and certainly didn't hold back. I really got into the rugby and played every Saturday for the rest of the season in the fourth team on the wing. It wasn't a very high standard of rugby, which suited me, being so new to playing it, but that meant me being stuck out on the wing and rarely getting the ball, which was a bit boring.

In the second season, after three or four matches, we found ourselves away to Finchley at their ground. Our hooker got injured, and he had to go off. The captain got us all together and asked, "Who wants to move to Hooker?" I was freezing stuck out on the wing, and all I could see was this steam rising from the scrums that looked nice and warm. My hand was the first to go up.

The props showed me what to do, and after banging heads with the opposite hooker a few times, much to his anger, I got the hang of it. It was far better than standing alone out on the wing watching the game like a spectator. In our next match, we were away to a team. They had a small, stocky kid playing scrum half. He was a few inches shorter than me but very fast around the scrum and all over the pitch. He had a nasty streak and kept punching our players on the sly behind the ref's back. As we broke from a scrum, one of my props said, "We should whack that little fucker." As I came alongside the scrum half, I did a nice little quick righthand punch flush to the side of his jaw. He went face first into the mud.

When they realised what had happened, the ref got us all together and their linesman came running over saying, "I saw it – it was your hooker that hit him."

The ref, who was our ref, pulled me to one side and said, "No more of that, or I'll send you off." To my surprise and dismay, after about ten minutes of getting treatment at the side of the pitch, the scrum half came running back onto the pitch, and as he ran past me, he winked at me. The rest of the match I got stamped on and kicked at every opportunity by the whole of their team, but I accepted it, and as we walked off the pitch I shook hands with them all, including the scrum half, who said he hadn't been hit so hard in all his life, and we both laughed.

I remained at hooker for the rest of the season. Whilst playing rugby, I had also been going to a swimming pool to help with my fitness. I think it was every Thursday they had lane swimming for adults. I always opted for the slow lane and plodded along up and down, doing a nice, easy breaststroke. This one night when I got back to the shallow end where I could touch the end and stand up for a bit of a breather, there were three young lads in their late teens or early twenties just standing there, splashing water at each other and messing about.

I said, "Oi! You fucking idiots. You are supposed to be lane swimming, and you are stopping people from getting to the end and having a breather." Instead the people – and some of them were quite elderly – would have to just turn around before getting to where these idiots were standing, which was some three or four metres away from the end. One of them said something smart back, and I said, "I'll knock all three of you out in a minute."

What I hadn't realised was the lifeguard had come down and was standing just to the left of me on the side of the pool. He said, "I'm afraid you will have to leave now."

I said fine, and I got out of the pool. I said, "I may just be waiting for you three when you leave later."

I didn't wait, I just went home, and when I told my mate in the pub that weekend, he just laughed and said, "Roger, you must be the only person I know who can get into a fight in a swimming pool." It did seem quite strange and not a good location to have a fight.

I was working with a couple of friends who were both one year older than me. They were both bricklayers, and they had another good friend as their labourer. The two of them were right characters. I'll call them No. 1 and No. 2. The job they asked me to help them with was in North London. It was a massive old house they were extending. Because I lived outside West London, they gave me the company transit van. I could then drive in each morning and pick them all up, apart from the labourer, who drove his own car each day.

We got into a nice little routine with me going to pick up the first one, then on to No. 1's flat, where he would always be just getting out of bed. His wife was running around the flat, picking things up and chatting to us, as she was a real diamond and a nice person. We would eventually get to the site and start on the brickwork. The labourer was very funny and had a lot of fingers in a lot of pies. We were always taking the piss out of each other and particularly testing each other's bottle. The labourer had quite a long handle to his plastic hod, and I used to wind him up that proper hoddies would cut it off and have a short handle. He went on about how sacred his hod was to him and that no one touches it, etc.

One day he went down to the café, and I got his hod and climbed up to the top scaffolding, then shinned a twenty-one-foot pole up onto the roof and put the handle of his hod down the chimney pot, leaving just the actual hod showing. This was very dangerous and a mad thing to do so high up. I was shaking but also laughing at the same time. When he came back and we returned to work, he couldn't find his hod anywhere. No. 1 and No. 2 were winding him up for about an hour: "How can you lose your hod?" He was getting madder and madder, then No. 1 pointed up to the highest chimney and said, "What's that up there?" His face was a picture. We all fell about laughing, and he couldn't believe how it got up there. He started to climb up to get it, but he couldn't get all the way, so I had to step in as I was worried he may fall, and that would not have been funny. I returned it, and he said, "Roger, you are fucking mental."

Early in the mornings driving the van, I would cut down a short one-way road, going the wrong way, as it saved a very long way around and it was always empty that early. On one morning there was a policeman there, and I put my foot down and drove as fast as the old van could go, all the way to work. When I picked up No. 2 and told him the policeman may have got my number, he laughed, but then he said, "Shit, Rog, this van is stolen." Apparently, they had been given the van by an old mate who was going to get it crushed. They were desperate to do this job and didn't have any other transport. We had to have a big meeting when we got to No. 1's flat. We didn't go to work that day. I got the train home, and they had the van crushed. I drove my wife's car for the last few weeks to get the job finished. We all went our separate ways after that job. I think No. 1 went back to working with cars, as that was his original trade. The labourer got a job on another site, and No. 2 is now doing life in prison for murder.

Shortly after this, someone I knew asked me to price up some works to an old shop-type building in Old Bond Street in London's West End. It was just building several six-inch-thick block walls on various floors inside the building, while they renovated it into new exclusive jewellers. Me and my mate went there for about one week, and we got it all done by 1:00 p.m. on the Friday. The main man paid me my £2,000. I paid my mate £500, leaving the remaining £1,500 to me. A nice little earner for one week's work.

We were feeling very happy with ourselves and decided to have a stroll around the corner into Piccadilly Circus for a couple of beers before going home. As we walked up Great Windmill Street, this scouse fella approached us and said, "If you are looking for a beer, lads, with some lovely ladies dancing for you, give me a tenner for this ticket, and it will get you into that bar across the road." I thought, why not, let's have a giggle, and I gave him the £10. We handed the ticket to this bloke sitting behind a glass screen, beside the door to this club. As we entered this dark and dingy club, I noticed three old ladies sitting at the bar, the youngest being about sixty years old. There was a small dance area with one pole going from floor to ceiling in the centre. I ordered two bottles of Budweiser at the bar, but the barman said, "You have to sit at a table as it's waitress service only, and you must buy the waitress a drink. It's the house rules."

We sat at a small round table, and we were the only customers in the bar. This old waitress came over and said abruptly, "What do you want?" I ordered two bottles of Budweiser once again. She came back with the two bottles of Bud and left a bill on the table. I looked at it, and it was for £15, £5 each for the Buds and £5 gratuity. I put £15 on top of the bill on the table, then asked, "When do the sexy ladies start dancing, then?" This waitress replied, "When it's full, probably about 7:00 p.m." I looked at my watch, and it was only 1:30 p.m. I turned to my mate and said, "This is bollocks."

I walked out and back across the road to the scouse fella. I hit him with a straight right punch, and he hit the floor but managed to scamper up and run inside the doorway and up the stairs.

I shouted after him, "Come back here, you wanker, and give me my tenner back, you scumbag!"

I heard him shout back, "Fuck off. The boys will get you for this."

As I walked back out of the doorway and into the street, my mate was there, having followed me out of the bar. This bloke from a nearby market stall came over to me and said, “You boys better scarper. The heavy mob will be here in a few minutes, and they don’t fuck about.” We quickly walked off down a side road. We did look over our shoulder a couple of times, though. We got back to my van and drove home.

Chapter Seven
Living in Bandit Country

I was struggling at home. I just couldn't keep up with all the bills and the expense. I was working seven days a week, and I didn't see much of my son growing up, as he was in bed when I left early for work in the mornings, and he was in bed when I got home late from work in the evenings. By the time we got to 1988/89, the chancellor had announced he was removing the mortgage tax allowance for both partners as a couple. This caused the property market to crash, and a recession was just around the corner. My wife had already decided she wanted to go back to live in Ireland. We went over there on a short holiday and we found a plot of land, and it had planning permission to build a house on it. We bought a mobile home to put on the land, to live in whilst I built the new house, my wife was very happy. The location was in a very republican area. I must point out, the Irish people do not call it 'bandit country'. That was the British soldiers who called it that, and the Irish republicans just played along with it. There were many deaths carried out in other parts of Ireland, but they would transport the bodies to be found there, just to add to the infamy.

I got started on building the new house. We had already instructed an architect to produce the drawings, and they were approved by building control. I got ground workers to start putting in an access road from the main road up to the position of where the new house would stand. Our location was out in the country, surrounded by fields and very close to the border with Southern Ireland. The nearest town was fifteen minutes driving northwards. That's where the builders merchants were located, and I could get some of the materials for our building project. Being in this environment in 1989 was a bit scary for someone with my cockney accent; luckily, having relatives there helped a lot. Her family were very helpful, and they knew a lot of people.

To fit in properly with the locals, I went to the boxing club in the town. As soon as I got talking to the main trainer, he accepted me with open arms, and he was so pleased to have someone with my boxing experience arrive at his club. On one of my trips back to London, I called into the Lonsdale sports shop in Hammersmith – it was run by my old boxing friends Len and Dennie Mancini – as I used to get my boxing gear from there over many years. The Mancinis had spent their whole lives in boxing, as managers, trainers, and even promoters for many years. I explained about being at this small club over in Ireland, and Len went downstairs and brought up lots of old boxing posters with names in red and blue ink from old boxing shows in Lime Grove Baths and Harringay Stadium. Many great boxing names on them from the 1950s, '60s and '70s. He said, "Here. Take these back with you for the gym walls." That's just how generous the boxing family were, and Len and Dennie were good people.

I also popped over to see Charlie Magri in his new sports shop on Bethnal Green Road. Charlie was terrific, and he gave me a poster of his first world title fight. He signed it, then he gave me about a dozen small signed photos, for me to give to the kids when I got back to Ireland. The Irish kids were over the moon and the trainer thanked me. The trainer then did me a big favour by putting me in the local paper. It explained Roger from London has joined the boxing club to help with the training, and it explained about my experience and fighting a former world champion. It went on to mention my father being an Irish tunnel man.

I noticed the difference after the paper was sold in the shops; everyone was saying hello to me more often, and even the other builders were now talking to me more. I still met the odd IRA man in the town's pubs. One man was a very serious individual. When I explained I was just a cockney bricklayer, he replied, "Well, we'll see that after you've laid the first brick, won't we?" but I wasn't bothered as I knew my brickwork well. There were many scary times, but most of it was my paranoia. One time British soldiers landed a helicopter in one of our fields, and about ten soldiers jumped out and started to walk over the fields looking through the grass with their rifles. Two of them came up to me. I was laying bricks at the time, and I had the front of the house up to about three feet high.

The first soldier got out a notebook and asked me some questions. You should have seen his face when I replied in my cockney accent – he nearly fainted. Who would expect to come across a London brickie in the middle of a field, and here of all places? When I explained I was married to a local girl, they became a lot colder towards me and very abrupt. One of them said, "What's in that old barn over there?"

I replied, "nothing but straw, I think."

They made me go with them to the barn. I had to open it while they stood back several yards waiting for a booby trap explosion. They walked in and put their guns through the straw, and there was an old door under it. They stood back again and made me lift open the door, but it had just been laid flat on the earth. I picked it up, and then when we cleared more straw there were more doors, but they had all just been laid to cover the earth. The only thing under them were the worms. The soldiers were happy now, and their helicopter took them away, but what I hadn't realised was they had left two of their soldiers behind in the corner of the top field. They were digging a hole at the highest point of my land. I approached them and asked them what they were doing. I had my Staffordshire bull terrier, Jack, with me.

They replied, "We are setting up an OP (observation point). We'll be here for a couple of nights, then we'll be gone. You better keep that dog tied up, or we'll put a bullet in it."

I walked away and left them to it. They were gone two days later. The boxing trainer asked me if I'd like to box on the coming Saturday afternoon in an exhibition bout in a place just a few miles away. He told me I would be getting in the ring with the current Ulster middleweight champ. I said, "Okay, why not? It'll be fun."

I drove on my own to the location. I got changed, and I was in the ring a few moments later to have an exhibition with the Ulster champion. There was quite a crowd there for a daytime show on a Saturday. I went through the three rounds very easily, and at one point the trainer told me to hold back a bit, or I'd be upsetting the crowd. The bout finished, and we shook hands. The ref held both our hands up. Then the trainer said, "Stay in the ring, Rog. I think they want you to do another bout."

The all-Ireland light-middleweight champion's opponent had failed to turn up, and they asked if I could stay in the ring and take him through three rounds for the crowd. I was happy to accommodate him. He was much taller than the middleweight I had just boxed, and he was a good mover. In the third round, he started to get a bit flash and caught me with a couple of good shots. I responded by putting him on the floor with a left hook, and the crowd booed. My trainer shouted at me to back off. I carried him for the rest of the round, and when it finished, again the ref held both of our hands up. When I left the ring and walked back to the changing room, I heard a few of the locals saying, "He's just an arrogant Brit." I got changed and shot off very quickly.

When I got back to my land, my wife told me that my father was here. He had gone off into the town on his own for a drink. He had just turned up and my wife had collected him, then dropped him into town before she returned to the mobile home. It was a wonderful surprise. I drove into town, and there he was holding court at the bar in the main pub. He had them all enthralled with his funny stories. I knew a few of the locals in his company; they were congratulating me on having a great dad. We stayed for another hour, then I drove him back to my mobile home and let him sleep the beer off in my bed. I was very happy to see my father and for him to see what I was doing on my own. He was the only member of my family to ever see it. Next day I drove him to his old hometown village out in the mountains, heading west for three hours. I left him there and drove back. When I went to the boxing club the following week, the trainer asked me if I'd do an exhibition bout in Belfast at a boxing club. I said okay, and on the following Sunday I was driving my little escort van with the boxing trainer in the passenger seat and several of our junior boxers in the back of the van. When we arrived on the edge of the estate where the boxing club was located, I noticed black flags hanging from every lamppost. The trainer explained to me how last week a youngster had been shot by a British soldier with a rubber bullet and died. We came up to a British army stop point. They made us all get out of the van, and they put a dog into it to search it. I tried to make small talk with the soldiers, but they just ignored me. They waved us through, and as we approached the gym there were lots of people walking towards a large church for Sunday mass. They all looked very relaxed. Then we arrived at the boxing club. I was very relaxed also. After all, it was just a gym fight and an exhibition of three rounds.

When we entered, I was shocked to see it was absolutely packed with people and smoke. I was introduced to the main trainer and shown over to some chairs beside a wall, where me and the other boxers had to get changed with everyone looking at us. He asked me if I'd like to warm up on the punch bag first, then pointed over and said, "That's the lad you'll be boxing against today."

I looked over and saw this boxer doing pull-ups on a high bar with no shirt on. His six-pack had a six-pack, he was sweating loads, and he looked a bit bigger than me all around. The people made a circle by moving back from the bag to allow me to punch it. It was strange to have all these eyes on me while on a punch bag, and I could hear them muttering, but I couldn't make out any words. The reason they were all there was the main trainer had been building it up all week by telling everyone I was one of the best English boxers and that I had fought many big names in boxing, and that I had just beaten the Ulster champion and the all-Ireland light-middleweight champion, which was of course all nonsense as they had only been exhibition bouts.

I got in the ring and looked at the other boxer, who was snarling at me. I thought I may be in a bit of trouble here. The other boxer was indeed a good bit bigger than me, and I found out later he would be going to the Commonwealth Games to represent Ireland at middleweight. A buzzer went, and we were off, sizing each other up with the usual couple of jabs. Then he upped the pace and took the centre of the ring. I then took a few very good combinations from him, and I didn't really know where I was. Boy did he hit hard. I got through the next two rounds using all my experience just to hang on to him, then halfway through the third round, he did me with a good body shot and I couldn't breathe. I went down on one knee for a few seconds to get my breath. To his credit, he backed off, and then I got up and continued taking more of his punches. When the final buzzer went, his trainer held up his arm in victory, which was cheered loudly by the people, who within ten minutes had vacated the gym, leaving it empty. I got changed wondering, *what was that all about? I'm twenty-nine years old and well past my best.* We stayed for some of our young lads to spar, then drove away from Belfast. The trainer sitting beside me said to me on the journey home, "It was a good job you let him win, or it may have got nasty in there." I looked at him, and then we both burst out laughing as we usually did.

The next boxing show we went to was in Derry (Londonderry to the Protestants). I wasn't boxing, just helping in the corner as a second to the main trainer. We were in my escort van with me driving, the trainer in the passenger seat, and two of our young boxers in the back. It was very dark on the country roads, and I had no idea where we were as the trainer was directing me, and he knew the roads like the back of his hand. We came across a red light in the road ahead, and he told me to slow right down. Usually a red light was British soldiers doing roadblocks and checking on vehicles or people. I had been told when I first arrived in Northern Ireland to have my British driving license handy for the RUC, UDR, or British soldiers and my Irish passport handy for anyone else. As we approached slowly, the trainer said, "This time, Rog, you're going to need your Irish passport."

As I lowered the window, this man in a soldier's uniform said in a very strong Irish accent, "We are the Irish Republican Army. Do you have any ID, please?" I gave him my Irish passport. He looked at it closely, then said, "Where would you be going to?"

The trainer lent over and said, "We're from the local town, and we are just taking the boys to a boxing show near the Bogside in Derry."

To my relief, he handed me back my passport and said, "That's fine. Have a good night," and we drove on, passing a soldier in the ditch to my right with the biggest gun I had ever seen. I would have to admit that I was shaking a bit and kangarooing the van along the road as my legs were trembling. The trainer told me later the man in the ditch had an ArmaLite rifle. He went on to say it was very rare for that to happen, and they must be looking for someone in particular. We had a good night at the show, with two winners, and a nice, clear drive home.

It's funny how your mind plays tricks on you, and I was guilty of paranoia on a few occasions whilst living there in the fields. One time I had been out having a beer with a couple of locals I got to know, and it got to that time to go home. They invited me back for a game of cards to one of their houses in the middle of nowhere, about three miles from my place. I wasn't much of a card player, and when we got there, they said they would be playing poker and got out great wads of money. I said, "I'll just watch if that's okay."

These were big men with big heads of black hair and strong accents. I could hardly make out what they were saying at times. They had plenty to drink, and bottles of whiskey were on the table. There was a bit of shouting and back slapping, but it was all in good humour. It got to about 2:00 a.m., and I left in my escort van. I pulled out into the narrow country lane in the pitch black, and after about one mile a pair of strong headlights came out of a siding and someone was following me, lighting up my rear-view mirror with their bright lights. I shit myself!

There would usually not be anyone on these tiny lanes at this time. My first thoughts were the RUC, then my second thoughts were someone far more sinister. I tried to stay calm and not panic. They followed me all the way until I turned into my land, then they went past and continued. In the morning, I told my wife and she said, "That was probably someone making sure you got home all right." Now why didn't I think of that?

The following Sunday, we were in 11:00 a.m. mass at the town's Catholic church. It had been closed for a bit to get renovated, and now it was open and packed solid with people, with some even standing down the aisles. It now had a large window behind the altar. You could see through the glass to a large wooden cross with a statue of Jesus crucified on the cross, with nice flowers all around the bottom of the cross. It was quite dramatic and looked good. As mass continued, I noticed through the window someone outside near the cross in the church gardens. It became clear it was several Maroon Berets – British paratroopers – using their rifles to look through the flowers at the bottom of the cross. This was an obvious timing thing to show everyone they were there, like a show of strength to the Catholic community. When we left the church, they were all gone.

I was getting on well with the building of the house. I was using a nice brick, and the local building inspector said it was the best brickwork he had ever seen. I laid every brick that went into that house, apart from just one that I helped my son James lay. The house was just about done and our money had all gone. I wanted to find work there, but to do so I would've had to travel to Belfast, and my wife did not want that. She said, "It would be best for you to go back to England." That was the end of our marriage. It was heart-wrenching putting all my things into the back of my escort van, including our dog, Jack. It was the hardest thing I had ever done, saying goodbye to my son, but I assured him I would be over for visits and I would talk on the phone with him as much as I could. That was it, and I drove to Belfast to get the overnight ferry to Liverpool.

Chapter Eight
Back to London Once Again

I landed back with my parents, who were now living in a fourth-floor flat in West London, with a continuous balcony running along in front of the front door, and they had their own small balcony at the back of the flat off the living room. I apologised for just turning up and especially with the dog, but my parents were fine with it and welcomed me. I got in touch with the breeder I bought Jack from in Scotland, and he said he had a mate working away from home in West London. I met him on Friday, and he took the dog from me to go back to Scotland. I was very sad to lose a friendly dog and one that was full of character, but it was the best for him, and he was more important than me.

A friend of mine got me a start on a site with a couple of subbies I didn't know very well then, but as time went on I got to know them well, as they were from an area I knew a lot of people from, and they knew a lot about boxing as well. I wasn't in a good place mentally after returning from Ireland, where I had lived for just over a year in the middle of a field in a caravan. Over the next couple of years, I went through some torrid times, as divorce is not a nice thing to go through, especially with a young child who had to learn to live in a different place, and I mean *very* different from London. He had lost his dog and more or less lost his dad as well. I felt a crushing guilt about leaving him there, and here I was back in London, and believe me I was very angry inside. I met this girl from South London who was just as mad as me. We had a very passionate relationship. Many times, getting into fights with other people in pubs around South or West London. I was not good for her, and she certainly wasn't good for me, and it only lasted a few months.

I had all this anger bubbling away inside of my head. On the sites I used to ask a labourer to hold up a Thermalite building block, which was four inches thick. I would wrap a cloth around my right hand and then hit the block with a solid punch and break it in two. This was no mean feat, and others would just hurt their hands or say, "Fuck off. You must be mental to do that." I came a cropper, though, on one site, when I didn't realise we were using 7N blocks, which were far denser than the usual 3.5N blocks. I hit the block three times, breaking two knuckles and leaving the shape of my fist indented into the block. I had to walk away feeling like a right Toby (*Toby jug* is rhyming slang for *mug*).

One time this girl disappeared for a week. I couldn't get hold of her. It was like she had just disappeared. Then I got a call from her, and she was crying. She told me she had been kidnapped by her ex-husband, who was recently released from prison after doing many years for firearm offences. He had called her and arranged for her to go to his basement flat for a meeting. He knocked her about a bit before kicking her out. I was already aware of how mad he was, as she had told me that he had been thrown out of the army for his violence towards other soldiers. He then became a mercenary and went to Africa. She said, "He may come looking for you, as he told me he knew I was seeing an ex-boxer."

I told her not to worry about me, I'll see her sometime next week, I need some time to consider my options on what to do about this. I went to see an old friend and explained the whole thing to him and what I wanted to do about it. He asked me over and over again, "Are you sure this is what you want to do, Roger?" he then put me in touch with someone.

I went to see him and asked for a handgun. He asked me if it had to be clean (meaning it hadn't been used for any other crimes). I said, "Yes I would prefer a clean one." He replied, "That'll be a monkey, then." (A monkey is £500.) I said give me a few days to get the money, and I left. I called the girl and told her to phone up her ex and tell him that I would meet him, and we could sort this all out. An hour later she called me back and told me she had rang him and told him I wanted to meet him, but she also told him I had recently returned from Northern Ireland, and I had a lot of connections in the IRA. This was of course not true. She had made it up to scare him.

This seemed to worry him, as his reply to her was, "Tell him to forget it and to fuck off. You are not worth it, you slag."

That was the end of that, then. I went back to see the man and I cancelled my order. I walked away and smiled. How stupid was I. I told one of my pals about it all, and he was mad. He said, "You were probably going to do life in prison or get killed for a girl you hardly know. Get a grip, Roger, for fuck's sake."

I became a supervisor for these subbies, and after the first project, I moved on to a big office development in the city. I met this bloke on site from New Zealand; he had arrived in London looking for labouring work, and I got him the start with me on this site. On one Friday after work, I went back to a pub with him, near to where he was living with his girlfriend. Coming straight from work and it being the summer, I was wearing just shorts and a vest. My kiwi mate's girlfriend turned up, and I met her for the first time. She was also from New Zealand. After a few more pints, lots of these kiwis were coming into the pub and seemed to be celebrating a birthday or something. It was just a short walk from the pub and would I like to go with them? I said, "Okay, why not?" This flat was up above a shop, and to access it you had to go down an alley alongside the shop, and up a rear fire escape's metal stairway. There was a large New Zealand flag hanging out of the window up above the shop, for everyone to see on the busy road. It got quite late, and we had a good time. I had spoken to only a couple of kiwis that seemed a bit standoffish, and it was obvious my mate and his girlfriend were more welcome than me. As we left around 1:00 a.m., we had to squeeze along the hallway past people standing, drinking with their back to the wall, to squeeze past. The lady whose birthday and party it was kissed both my mate and his girlfriend goodbye. I put my hand out to shake hers to say goodbye to her, but she snarled at me and said, "Well, I hope I don't see you again, with all your muscles and tattoos. I hate you cockneys."

I was shocked after such a pleasant night. What could I say? Then this big kiwi standing next to this lady started to laugh. Now I knew what to do, and I hit him with a solid right, and his head hit the wall behind and he slid to the floor out cold. It was like someone had pushed an emergency button, as the whole flat went into chaos. The kiwis must have been waiting for this to happen as they jumped on me from everywhere.

I started hitting anyone near me, but they got on top, as there was about thirty of them all trying to hit me. I put my arms in front of my face like a boxer does, when covering up from a deluge of punches on the ropes. All I could feel was the pitta, patta of fists hitting me, but they were very weak punches, and I was laughing behind my arms. They worked me out of the flat, and I fell down the metal stairway on my shoulder and felt a few kicks coming in as I slid all the way down to the bottom of the stairway and onto a rear dark road.

We continued with me covering up. Then the punches would stop, and I would open up again with my own hooks and straight punches. We got out into the middle of the road, and I saw four police Sherpa vans, with two north of me and two south of me, spread across the road, blocking it. It was hands-up time, and they threw me into the back of a police van along with my mate, who had spent the whole time trying to drag the kiwis off me. On the drive to the police station, I noticed I had blood coming from a split lip, and it was really split, right through the top left. It must have happened when I hit the metal stairs, as none of their punches could have caused it. When we got to the police station, I noticed they had only lifted the two of us and no one else. I had a go at the desk sergeant.

"Why haven't you lifted any of those other kiwis? It was thirty onto one."

He looked at me and shook his head and said, "If you want to go around fighting thirty kiwis on your own, best of luck to you, son. We heard you started it all."

We got put into an interview room, and they questioned us about what had happened. They said I would have to wait all night until the morning for a doctor to look at my lip.

We weren't being arrested, so I said, "I'm not waiting here all night. Let's go to my mate."

The policeman warned me, "If you go back there and we get called out again, you'll be nicked big time."

The two of us left the station and said goodbyes at the top of the road that went down past their flat. My mate lived just farther along past the shops. I now had to walk the length of road to get to my parents' flat, and you know what that meant: walking right past the kiwis' squat with their stupid flag hanging out of the window.

It was about 3:00 a.m. and deathly quiet. I just couldn't walk past and do nothing. I went quietly up the rear stairway and into the small kitchen. I went through the drawers looking for a knife to arm myself for a better defence, but all the drawers were empty.

I thought, *how do these people live like this?* I went into the large front room, and there were about six bodies sleeping, and a couple in sleeping bags. I kicked every one of them and said, "Get up, you wankers, and fight me one to one, not thirty to one."

They let out a couple of screams, then stood up and ushered me out into the kitchen beside the rear door. The girl who had started it all was full of apologies: "I am so sorry, I didn't think it would get so out of hand. Please forgive me. We don't want any more trouble."

I just laughed and looked at the wimps behind her hanging their heads, so as not to meet my eyes. I said, "Okay, let's leave it, then," as I walked out and down the metal stairway. I was happy that I had made my point, and in my own mind I had won the day. The following day, Saturday, I had to be at the site and work until 1:00 p.m. I had only had two hours of sleep.

There is a funny twist to this recollection. A bloke on the site said I should get my lip seen to, as it was a very deep cut and it went right through the lip, with the lip split in two. I walked along the road behind the site to the nearest hospital. I was seen by a young doctor in a white coat who said, "That looks nasty. Let's see if we can get some stitches into it."

Just then, an older man walked by, and the doctor called him in to have a look at my lip. This older man was an off-duty surgeon of some repute apparently. After studying my lip inside and out he said, "We'll soon sort that out," and he put on a white coat and a pair of gloves and set to work, stitching inner and outer stitches to the wound. He told me if it wasn't done properly, I would end up with a big lump on my lip. He did a fantastic job, and to this day you can hardly notice the scar on my lip.

Here's the twist: not only was he off-duty and he did it in his own free time on a Saturday morning, but he was also from New Zealand. How about that for not generalising about people from a country? I had met a bunch of kiwi idiots a few hours earlier, and now a true kiwi gentleman.

Shortly after this, my bosses promoted me to a visiting contracts manager. I had managed to save some money, and I bought a ground-floor flat outside West London and not far from a good rugby club. I went back to drinking in a pub in West London. A lot of the men working with me were from there. It was packed at the weekends with the odd celebrity coming in, as well as proper faces (old-school villains).

Due to my fragile mental state at this time, I got involved in the use of cocaine. I was very lucky in the sense that I never did it to get any sort of kick from it, but I managed to associate it with being able to drink and party longer. This is a very important difference, as I had friends who couldn't even come out to the pub without snorting half a gram of Charlie – cocaine. They would enter the pub already sweating and hyperactive. With me, it was after four or five pints, then "Where's the Charlie?" because it put you right back to if you had just arrived.

Imagine drinking ten pints. Most of us would be sitting in the corner dribbling after that, but if you had taken Charlie, you'd be bouncing around the pub having a laugh, and a lot of people I knew were on it, so the whole pub would be rocking, and of course the girls loved it as well. There were plenty of my mates and some people I mixed with who wouldn't touch it. They hated it; they were the sensible ones. Don't blame the pub as they tried everything to stop the use of drugs in their establishment, but users were very clever and could go outside and around the corner to do it, then come back into the pub. We also drank in another pub just down the road.

At this time in my life (just into my thirties), I knew an awful lot of big-time villains, and quite often someone would say, "Rog, many people don't realise just how many serious people you know."

I knew the top men from most areas of London, and some from Essex and Kent, too. This gave me a good standing in the pub. Many of my mates also knew some of the same people. Around 1991, we had a bit of bother in the pub. As in any London pub, we'd get all sorts of people coming in and out, many tourists and strangers, but we just had our own little clique at the end of the bar, and we kept ourselves to ourselves.

One day someone I did not know came in and shot another man I also did not know with a sawn-off shotgun. I was standing about ten feet away from the man who got shot. You do not want to be that close to something like that happening; the noise from the gun was deafening, and I had tinnitus for several weeks afterwards with constant ringing in my ears. Like everyone else, I left the pub very quickly. I have no idea whatever happened to the victim or the shooter; they were both in and out of my life in about three minutes.

We had a bricklayer friend who was a real character, and I still haven't met anyone who could outdrink him. He would sit amongst us at the pub table and put his hand up to his forehead vertically, then move it forwards saying, "We are just passing through," and we'd all fall about laughing. He got killed by a bloke who he had fallen out with a few times. This bloke put a butcher's long meat fork right through him and out through his back, killing him. Whenever we met up in the pub sometimes, we'd all do the same action and say, "We are just passing through," as a tribute to our long-lost mate.

A week after the shooting, I was running a site not far away. On the Friday after work, we all went to the pub for the usual session of drinking. As the night went on, there were some lads we didn't know getting very loud and a bit nasty towards a few people. One of them approached me and said, “You’re supposed to be a tough guy in this pub. Try hitting me in the stomach, then I’ll hit you.”

I told him to go away and don’t be silly; he was the same size as me and looked just as strong. He kept persisting.

I eventually said, “Okay, but you hit me first, then I’ll hit you.”

He was delighted with this. I stood with my back against the bar so I couldn’t move backwards and said, “Give it your best shot.”

He drew back his arm and punched into my six-pack, but it held firm, and I said, “Right. My turn now.”

His face went white, but fair play to him, he said, “Go on, then.”

I stood very close to him, and I just swivelled my hips and hooked my right hand upwards through his solar plexus. I tried to get my fist to come out through his back. He hit the floor and could not breathe. They carried him out, and we all laughed and carried on drinking.

After about one hour, this young lad came back into the pub and straight up to me. He said, “You just made me look silly, so I need to fight you outside now.”

I tried to talk him out of it, and I offered to buy him a pint to forget about it, but he was determined he wanted to fight me outside. Some of my friends were pleading with him to drop it, as he wouldn’t stand a chance. I was getting angry now with all the fuss, and I said, “Fuck it, let’s get outside now, then.”

I walked him to the door, but he then put both arms up against the door frame to stop himself from going outside. It was like a comedy now, with me trying to push him out and a couple of my mates and him trying to stay inside the pub, as he had changed his mind.

What I hadn’t realised was the bar staff had called the police to come. Because it was only one week after the shooting incident, the police came in numbers and arrived in two vans. They came in from the top end of the pub and walked down through the pub towards us. I was pulled to the bar by an old villain who said, “Rog, stay here with me and don’t move.”

I stood alongside him and watched as all the police started talking to everyone. I looked over and saw this lad laughing with a policewoman. She was standing on one side of a table and he was on the other side of the table, with another table and chairs behind him. I said to my old pal beside me, “I’m not having that.”

I walked over between a couple of policemen and said to the policewoman, “Excuse me,” and I nudged her out of the way, then bang! I hit him with a great straight right punch. He went backwards over the table behind him, and he was out cold.

Then chaos erupted. Two policemen and this policewoman grabbed hold of my arms, but I just locked them and started to move them, with the coppers swinging about holding on to my arms. It was like something out of the Keystone Cops' silent movies. Then one smart copper bent down behind me and got hold of both of my ankles and pulled them off the ground. I went face down onto the floor, and they all sat on me.

They threw me into the back of a police Sherpa van, my face flat on the metal ridged floor with hands cuffed behind my back. All I could see was coppers feet, and one of them stamped onto the back of my head and said, "Not so tough now, are you son?"

I said nothing, because if there was one thing I had learnt from all my times involved with the police, it was to keep quiet and say nothing. This was their kingdom and their show. The driver kept driving around and around and then stamping his foot onto the brakes, making my face, with a policeman's size-fourteen boot on it, slide up and down the metal floor, which hurt. I knew it was only a five-minute drive to the police station, and yet it seemed like an age to get there. The van stopped, and I expected to be getting dragged out, but instead I heard the back doors open, then this weight landed on to my back.

They had circled back to the pub and thrown one of my good friends into the van on top of me. His crime was telling the police as they left the pub, "He hasn't got a mark on him when you took him, and we want to see him in the morning, to make sure he still hasn't got any marks on him."

They whacked him and threw him into the van onto my back. When we arrived at the police station, they dragged my friend out first by the handcuffs, and he had a nasty gash under his chin. I made sure I got my feet down first onto the tarmac before they lifted my head up to walk into the back of the police station. We were both charged with causing an affray.

I asked a policeman who lived not far from me if he could have a look at the case. He said no he couldn't do that, but he could tell me that a charge for 'causing an affray' is like a train with lots of carriages, and a brief can get each of the carriages taken away depending on the circumstances, and as there were only two of you, that would be quite easy for a decent brief to do.

A few days later, he told me, "By coincidence, I was in the police station where you got nicked the other day, and I had a quick look at your CR number (criminal record file). Your file is under the heading 'Man of violence'."

He didn't have much to do with me after that conversation. I wasn't surprised, as good, law-abiding policemen should not mix with the likes of me. We appeared in the local magistrates' court a few weeks later. Our brief got the charges dropped to threatening behaviour, and we both got £50 fines and walked away. There were no charges for me hitting the bloke, as he wouldn't press charges, which was very decent of him.

The following week I went to a nightclub with a mate, who eventually slipped away and went home. I was at the bar, and this gorgeous older woman got very close to me, rubbing her breasts against me. I said hello, and we got talking, with her introducing me to her husband, who was sitting behind her on a bar stool. I bought them a drink, and they returned the favour, and they looked like quite a wealthy couple in their early fifties.

The man said to me, "Do you like stockings?"

I said, "What man doesn't?"

He then discreetly lifted his wife's skirt up to show me her black stocking tops, then lifted it a little higher to show me her shaved, smooth pussy.

I just nodded and said, "Very nice."

We carried on talking and ended up back at their house in a posh area. Their house was very nice, and they had fantastic furniture. He wanted me to fuck his wife whilst he sat and watched from nearby, then he got undressed and got into bed with us, and all three of us enjoyed sexual acts with each other. I can confirm I still would not let anyone near my arse, to me the arse is for one thing only, and it`s my opinion it should never be included in sexual activity. It was a strange experience and afterwards I was very confused thinking about the three of us together.

I certainly learnt a lot about myself from that first experience of being with two people at the same time. It also gave me a great insight into what women had to put up with sexually from men. This came in very handy when I spoke with women, as they thought I was very understanding, and of course after this I was much better at sexual acts with them, as I was far more sensitive to their needs. I would like to thank that first couple for opening my eyes up to sex I had never encountered before. Although it seems, where I get mixed up and confused sexually is when you put love into the mix – then everything becomes very different. I have always had problems with the two, and how to keep them separate, or how to embrace them both in a loving relationship. How do you differentiate between the act of true lovemaking, and the very different, lustful erotic sex?

Maybe because of the life I had led, I seemed to completely misunderstand the difference between love and sex. It made me think of all the times I had been in the company of old-school villains, many of them a lot older than me, and some of them would have a younger bloke with them, who they would introduce as their 'northern friend' or 'young companion'. I was aware of the term 'prison bent' when you were in prison for a lot of years. Some villains would partake in some sexual activity with their own sex, but it would be very limited and only used as a quick fix for immediate pleasure. When coming out of prison, they would go back to women only. The odd one would be naturally gay, and when freed would stick with the company of young men. A serious villain once explained to me that having any sort of sex with a man, and sometimes it may be just oral, was a statement of how tough they were. As in, "I can do this, you cannot." I understood that way of thinking, which I suppose is quite shocking really. I should have just dismissed it. I found myself getting turned on by this recent liaison with the married couple, and I made contact through a local contact mag with another couple. It was a real turn-on having a certain amount of power over them; it was a new world I had known nothing about. The men were happy to be cuckolded, and the women seemed to like my body, and they loved to show off in front of their man. I only did it a few more times, as I started to feel I was being used, as much as I was using them. I turned to the comfort of nice older women over the next few months, and sex with them was terrific. I really got turned on by their stockings, especially if they were tan coloured, and by their thick white bras and large breasts. I also had a thing about girdles as well; that may have come from my early days as a child and seeing my mother in them.

Some months later, someone I knew had organised a rave at a nightclub in the city. This club was owned by some very serious people you did not mess with. It was to be a rave from 9:00 p.m. to 9:00 a.m., and it was £10 a ticket, and one week before Christmas. The organiser asked me to stand at the bottom of the stairs, and as people entered and walked down the stairs to the reception desk, they handed their ticket to the girl, who then tore the ticket in half. As the person would then turn left to go through the doors to the rave, I would be standing in front of the doors, and they could not go past me without showing me the half a ticket.

I asked, "Why would you need me there, when the club has its own bouncers?"

My friend replied, "Because I think the bouncers will be letting people in for fivers and pocketing the money."

He offered me £150 cash, and I accepted it. On the night of the rave, I turned up at about 8:00 p.m., one hour before opening, I was wearing black overcoat, black shoes, trousers, a white shirt, and no tie. I looked quite smart, and whilst driving there, I thought, *talk about poacher turned gamekeeper. This is a new one, with me on the door.* But then, it was to catch bouncers thieving, so I excused myself. I introduced myself to the club bouncers, and I was the smallest one by far. They asked, "What's your history, then?"

I replied with as much confidence and nastiness as I could, "I'm Roger the boxer, and I'll go through brick walls if I have to. I've been asked by the organisers to make sure you lot are not letting anyone in for cash. No one goes past me without half a ticket."

They smiled and said, "That's fine, Rog, we wouldn't do that."

The night started, and there were hundreds of people coming down the stairs and showing me their half of a ticket. I had never been to a rave before, and I knew nothing about them. I was surprised there was no alcohol being sold, just water behind the bar. When I did walk through the rave to the club toilets, it was very loud, with thundering music beating out, and packed with sweating people. There were women in the gents, and men going in and out of the ladies, but I just ignored it as that was not my job. Some girls were dancing topless, which was a nice bonus. I was feeling a bit tired as the night wore on, and when we got to about 1:00 a.m., one of the bouncers offered me a line of cocaine to pep me up a bit, which I gladly took. After that, I was letting in anyone with or without a half a ticket. The bouncers were shouting down to me from the top of the stairs, "Rog, let these in, they are okay."

Clever bouncers. The organisers thanked me days later and said their takings were much higher than they expected, so everyone was happy.

To say that at this period of my life I was a very unbalanced individual would be an understatement. I had let myself become a very dangerous idiot. The sites were shut for the Christmas break, and I went on a drinking session with a couple of the faces from a well-known local estate. After a very long day, there were only three of us left, and we went down the steps to a nightclub. It was about 1:00 a.m. The door was shut. I knocked on the door, and three bouncers came out and said, "We are now closed."

I hated arrogant bouncers who would laugh at you, dismissing you like a bunch of kids. We left and went to a local small club. Whilst drinking I was still mad inside with the bouncers. I finished my drink and said I was off home.

One of my mates said, "Don't be going back to that club, Rog. Let it go."

I replied, "I'm going straight home."

What did I do? I walked straight back to the club we had come from earlier, and I went down the steps and banged on the door. One of the bouncers pulled back a viewing hatch, like you have in prison cells, and said, "Go home, we are closed."

I kicked the door and told them to come out and fight like real men. One bouncer came out. I knew this bouncer as he worked on our site. He approached me and said, "Rog, you've had too much to drink. Just go home – you've become a Charlie monster."

That was like showing a red rag to a bull, and I hit him with a couple of good punches. He bent forward from the punches, then grabbed me around the waist. I pulled back from him, and I yanked his black jacket over his head, ripping it. I started to put in some solid hooks to his side. The doors of the nightclub opened. I was expecting them to come out mob handed and give me a good hiding, but they just dragged their mate back inside and locked the doors again. I started to kick the doors, calling them all wankers.

One of the bouncers pulled back the viewing cover and said, "Go home. He said he's going to sort you out back at the site after Christmas."

I walked up the steps, and along came two police officers on the pavement. "Are you causing trouble, sir?" they said.

I replied, "No, I was just going home," and I hailed a cab, then left.

I now had a fortnight break over Christmas to think about this bouncer who was going to 'sort me out' when we returned to the site after Christmas. In my unbalanced mind, I had to get prepared. I said to myself, "The word is out – he has to go."

The next day I drove to where I knew there was a hunting shop. I went in and said I wanted to buy a crossbow for hunting. The man was very helpful and showed me a nice black one, saying, "This is the most powerful handheld crossbow on the market, by Barnett. It'll pin a rabbit to a tree from one hundred feet."

I said, "Okay, I'll take it, and I'll have one of these six-inch bowie knives as well."

I returned to my flat, and I thought I had better get some practice in with my new toys. I was firing the crossbow bolts into my dirty washing basket and doing a very bad impersonation: "Are you talking to me?" *Pow! Pow!* with the crossbow, then I'd follow up with the bowie knife – job done. This is how stupid I was then: I went out into my back garden and fired a bolt at my garden fence. As I pulled the trigger, the crossbow went up a bit, and the bolt went over my fence. The lady in the next garden was hanging out her washing, and the bolt went right between two of her sheets already hanging from the line, luckily about thirty feet away from her, and she didn't notice a thing.

I expect that bolt is still lodged in that fence today. I now had only five bolts left, so I went back to the laundry basket. Christmas was over, and it was time to face the music with this irate bouncer. I had a plan. I had a green holdall bag with the crossbow, bolts, and the bowie knife in it. I had packed a small case and put it into my car. I had withdrawn £600 that was for my next month's mortgage from the building society, and I had it in my pocket. My plan was to do the bouncer, then get a train to Heathrow and buy a last-minute standby ticket to New York. Then get from New York into Canada, where I had a friend. I would stay with him for a couple of days, then make my way up to northern Canada and start a new life.

I turned up at the site about 11:00 a.m. and went to my foreman's office. We chatted about what had happened at the nightclub, and I asked him, "What is the word on the site?"

He told me he had spoken with the bouncer chap. He went on to say, "The bloke was a bit upset but didn't seem too aggressive, but he had a mate with him who was a bit mad and wanted to do you."

I opened the bag and showed my foreman the crossbow and bowie knife.

He said, "Hang on, Rog. There's no need to go that far; let's just see what he has to say first."

I agreed with that, and we went up to the second floor of the building. This bloke and his mate came up to us, and I have to say he seemed very calm and not too mad to me. We spoke about the incident at the nightclub before Christmas, and he said all he wanted was an apology.

I was shocked and I said, "You just want me to say I'm sorry for hitting you and ripping your jacket?"

He replied, "Yes, and that will be the end of it."

I apologised, and then we shook hands, and I walked away with my foreman. I took my bag and left the site. There was a building society nearby, and I walked over and paid the money back into my account to cover my mortgage. I felt relieved, and I just smiled and walked back to my car. It just goes to show how life can surprise you at times. I had spent the two weeks over Christmas assuming we'd have this big set to, when he probably wasn't even thinking about it, as he probably had to deal with loons like me all the time. Mind you I'd like to have seen his face after my foreman told him and his mate what I had brought to the site in the bag and what I had come prepared to do.

I think we all had a lucky escape that day. I needed to sort myself out again and calm down. I had been worrying about having a HIV/AIDS test for a while now, due to my exploits with swinging couples over the past few months. I went to a local clinic, and I finally had the test done. When you go back to get your results, it's very frightening, as you just don't know. If they say positive, it will change your life forever. It seemed like an age sitting in that waiting room, with others in the same situation. It was all very embarrassing, and I just didn't know where to look. I was called in to a small room, when the lady said I was negative.

I could have jumped over the moon with relief. I asked her how accurate the test was, and she replied, "It's about 99.9% accurate."

I thought that'll do for me. I got out into my car, and it was like that TV scene of Del and Rodney, in *Only Fools and Horses*, when they take it in turns to scream in their van after getting a load of money at the auction for an old watch. I let out a "*Yes!*" and punched the air a few times. I vowed to myself then to keep my dick in my pants, and to find a nice girl to settle down with.

A month or so later, I met a girl who became very special to me. I knew her father, as I had built a bungalow for him in the mid-eighties. I had called him, as he was very good with plumbing and gas boilers, and I had a problem with the gas boiler in my flat. He sorted it out for me, and he wouldn't take any money for the work. We got chatting, and I told him I was at a bit of a loose end regarding girlfriends, and it had been on my mind to settle down, as I couldn't keep living as if I was in the Wild West. He suggested I take his daughter, Gabby, out, and maybe she could cheer me up.

I went around to his house to see Gabby, but she was all dressed up and just leaving, going to a wedding with her mother. We arranged for me to go out with her the following Saturday to a small club nearby with a mate of hers. The following weekend we had a great time out, and a friendship started that turned into a full relationship. After a few months, Gabby moved into my flat. She was from a Jewish family but not very religious herself. I treated her by booking us on to a trip on the *Orient Express* train for St Valentine's Day. We got onto the train at Victoria Station at 7:00 p.m., and it travelled all around the Kent countryside until midnight. We sat in the Queen Mother's favourite carriage. The meal was fantastic, and the food was heart shaped – how romantic. There were violinists playing music and serenading everyone through the train. Overall, it was a great experience.

We were very happy for a while, but it wasn't long before the recession started to bite, and I was laid off by the subcontractors I was working for, even though they had become good friends. I knew they had a business to run, but I still wasn't happy. I went into a depression and I just stayed in the flat. I was skint and Gabby, who worked as a typesetter, was looking after me. If I went out to the pub, I'd buy myself a drink and tell my pals I'd stay on my own as I wouldn't be able to buy them a drink back. Drinks still came my way from them, as they knew how to look after each other when it was needed – they were good people. One of them bought a computer game system from me, even though he had no use for it and he didn't need it. He did it just to give me some money. Another friend in the pub, his father used to work with my father in the tunnels.

Whilst sitting around in the flat feeling sorry for myself, I decided I wanted to learn to sing. Don't ask me why, I just did. I looked in the local paper, and there was a singing teacher advertising for new pupils. I phoned and spoke with this posh woman who gave me an appointment for 9:00 a.m. next morning, at an address about two miles away. Gabby dropped me off at this large detached property on her way to work, which meant I was there early, at 8:30 a.m. I wandered about a bit until it got to 8:45, when I knocked on this large front door. It seemed like ages before this large buxom woman opened the door and let me in, asking me to follow her into this large room with a bare polished wooden floor, a large black grand piano, and a large chandelier – all very grand, I thought.

The lady asked me some simple questions, and I explained I hadn't sung since junior school, when I was about ten years old. She sat behind the piano, and I stood beside it and leant my hand on the piano. She shouted at me, "Please do not touch the piano." I don`t know why, but this made me laugh. She didn't look very happy.

She snapped at me quite abruptly: "We can start with some simple scales to go through. See if you can match the sound of my keys with some la la la's. I did my best and la la la for all I was worth, but she just shook her head and said, 'No, no, no, that won't do. Let's try to do it by humming to the notes.'"

And off I went humming as best I could, but once again she was shaking her head. The lady closed the piano lid and said, "I'm very sorry, but I'm afraid it would take too long to teach you to sing and cost a vast sum of money. I will see you out."

She motioned with her outstretched arm for me to leave the way we came in, and there I was back outside this large front door, and it was only just turned 9:00 a.m. I thought about knocking on the door for a laugh and pretending I had just arrived for my singing lesson, but I didn't think she would see the funny side of it. I just walked home humming and la la la-ing to myself. I explained everything to Gabby that evening, and she thought it was all very amusing.

Then I said, "I want to try acting," as I fancied myself as a British tough-guy actor. In the local paper there was an amateur dramatic society advertising. I called the number, and a lady answered and told me, "At this time of year we are mostly doing pantomime, but you are welcome to come along this Sunday. I'm sure there is something we could find for you to help with."

Gabby drove me to this school hall about four miles away from our flat. I walked in, and there were about ten people milling about in front of a large raised stage. The lady I had spoken with on the phone approached me and introduced herself. Then she turned and shouted to everyone who I was, and they all just nodded and kept doing what they were doing.

However, I noticed a small man not far from us looking me up and down, then when we made eye contact, he did that very camp thing of turning his head and body away quickly. The lady said, "That's our director, Stephen. He can be a bit fickle at times."

They explained to me it was a family-orientated pantomime, and could I be a Roman soldier and stand at the side of the stage perfectly straight and upright.

I said, "I'm sure I can manage that."

I took up my position at the side of the raised stage, and after about an hour I was starting to feel a bit bored and tired. This camp little fella was running around shouting out silly things, when he suddenly stopped and raised his voice in my direction: “Stop, stop, stop! You at the side, you just do not fit in. It must be the way you are standing. It just won’t do.”

I said, “How can I be standing incorrectly? It’s just standing.”

He said, “No, no, no, you just do not fit in. It’s just not working for me. You will have to leave now.”

I said, “I’ll come down there and knock you out in a minute, you little cunt!”

The lady then cut in with a raised voice: “Oh no, we’ll have to call the police. Please, can you just leave?”

I walked off the stage and they had all frozen, like a spider sitting perfectly still, thinking you cannot see him.

I walked out of the door muttering to myself. “Fucking poncey wankers, they don`t know anything about proper acting.” I walked all the way home with my acting career over before it began.

Gabby tried everything to cheer me up and arranged a birthday party for me at the pub and suggested we both dress up to surprise our friends there. I got a proper clown’s outfit in red tartan, and she dressed as a witch. When we were crossing the road outside heading for the pub, some of our friends looked out of the pub window and said, “Look at this nutter coming across the road,” not realising it was me and Gabby dressed up. When we entered the pub, they all fell about laughing.

We had a great night with a good DJ and karaoke. It was packed with people – even some of my old friends from school came over to see me. It was great to see them. There was one very special moment when a friend of mine who had not long been out from a short stay in Wormwood Scrubs Prison came into the pub. He had his neck in a rigid brace and his arm in a sling with a plaster cast on it. He had been set upon by someone with a baseball bat whilst visiting his ex-wife. It was a case of mistaken identity. We took to the stage and sang, *I Will Survive*. I didn’t know if he was grimacing from the pain or from our singing, but the whole pub was cheering us anyway. I’ve kept in touch with him, and he’s doing very well.

After the weekend on the Monday night, Gabby was sorting out some of her old teddies. I picked one up that was like Biggles, with a leather waistcoat and cap on and flying goggles. She pulled it out of my hand and said, “That’s special to me – it was from my ex fiancé.”

Next morning when she had gone to work, I thought, *the word’s out – Biggles has got to go.* I walked to our nearest garage, and I bought a gallon of petrol in a fuel can, and I walked back home with it, laughing to myself. I did a bit of a ritual and placed Biggles in the centre of my garden on the grass. I dowsed him in petrol and then set fire to him, almost setting fire to myself at the same time, as the flames went up in the air but also along the grass towards me where I had spilt petrol. I got away from the flames and watched Biggles disappear in the flames to ashes. When Gabby came home from work that night, I told her what I did, and that Biggles had to go. To her credit, she was a bit upset, but she could also see the funny side of it.

Later that week, I found out from a mate that a good friend of ours was in hospital with a fractured skull and concussion. He explained that the two of them had been out in London's West End until about 1:00 a.m. As they were walking along Oxford Street trying to get a taxi home, they came across a man selling hot dogs from a cart. One of our mates said he only wanted a bread roll with no sausage, so our other mate decided to help himself to the sausages and took a handful, saying, "I'll have his sausages," and they both walked away with the seller shouting abuse at them.

They got about twenty minutes down the road when the mate who was walking ahead turned around to say something to the other one, who had been lagging well behind by about twenty metres. He noticed his mate was on the floor with blood coming from his head. They got him into an ambulance and to the local hospital. My mate said he had no idea what had happened, as he hadn`t seen anything or heard anything behind him as he walked. I spoke to an old friend who used to work the pavement in this area of the West End, and he told me, "That'll be the Maltesers. They run all the selling carts there. If a seller has any trouble, he rings a number and explains everything to the bosses, who then send out a car full of heavies with baseball bats to the location. They do it very discreetly by just cruising the car alongside, and one jumps out, whacks the offender, and then they are gone within a couple of minutes."

Luckily our mate made a full recovery with no lasting damage. A lesson learnt.

That following Sunday, I got a phone call from my sister with some tragic news. Her twenty-year-old son had been killed in a car crash. I went straight there and took her to the hospital to see him. It was the most difficult thing I had ever had to do. I really was devastated, along with my sister and her family. The funeral was very difficult but attended by hundreds of people as he was so popular.

In the week after the funeral, I was cutting a tree down in my garden in the afternoon. I had to do it in the daytime and midweek when all my neighbours were at work, because they had already told me I couldn't cut it down as it was protected. That meant nothing to me. The word was out, the tree had to go. I put down the chainsaw as I got a phone call from my sister, and she was very upset.

My nephew who had died in the car crash was owed two weeks' wages by his employers. My sister wanted her son's girlfriend and his baby girl to have the money, but the bastards had stopped the cheque, with the boss telling my sister, "Money is no good to him now."

My sister asked me if I could have a word with this boss for her; she gave me his address just outside London. I said, "Leave it to me."

I was wearing shorts and vest. I put the chainsaw into my van. I drove the hour drive, constantly thinking of what I was going to do to this evil man. I arrived at this boss's address. It was a posh-looking upstairs flat that had its own front door. I banged on the door, but there was no answer. This went on for several more times, then I noticed the upstairs curtain move. I went back to my van, and I got out the chainsaw. I started it up, and what a noise it made. I was just about to start cutting through the front door, when it suddenly opened. A small fat man went to speak, but I had already pushed him back into the doorway, and I ran him up the stairs.

I pinned him to the wall by his neck, and I told him who I was, that I was there to collect my nephew's money. He said, "I'll call my brothers. They are a firm out of Luton."

It's a funny feeling when you know you have right on your side. It gives you an invincible power. I said, "Call them now, then, and tell them they better come tooled up and I'll be waiting here for them."

I looked around the flat and thought I could take the TV, the hi-fi, and any cash he had in the place for my nephew. He then agreed he would drop the money he owed to my sister's house in a few days as cash in an envelope. I accepted that, as he was now shaking like a leaf, and I could see just how scared he was. A few days later, my sister rang me and thanked me as she had received the money owed to her son. I know it was only a small thing, but it felt good to have achieved something for her, after all that she had been through.

A short time after this, I decided to have a vasectomy reversal. I knew there were no guarantees that it would work. It was just something that I needed to do, to alter myself back to just simple old Roger, and put my body back to its original state. The operation was going to be difficult, and the surgeon told me afterwards there wasn't much of the tubes left to work with and to open back up, but he had managed it.

A few months later Gabby was having problems with her stomach. At first the doctors thought it was irritable bowel syndrome, but it wasn't. She learnt that she had Crohn's disease. This is a problem with your bowels not digesting food correctly, and it can be very painful. There is no known cure for Crohn's disease, and more and more young people are getting it, which is very sad. They sometimes cut a section of the bowel away, but they didn't want to do that in Gabby's case. They put her on strong painkillers and steroids, which meant she got larger in weight.

Not long after this, Gabby announced she might be pregnant. She bought a test kit, which showed she was indeed pregnant, and then she had a proper doctor's test that confirmed she was now carrying my child. We were very happy but equally very surprised, as she had been taking the pill. I decided at this time to speak to someone about my mental state and my violent behaviour.

The doctors sent me to my local mental health unit (MHU). I saw a very nice female psychologist, and we spoke for about an hour, then I went to see her every fortnight. They are very well trained to get everything out of you. She said very little, with just the odd short sentence like "And how did that make you feel?" or "And then what?"

When I returned to my flat after a session, I went straight to bed and slept soundly for hours. It really does take everything out of you when you unload your thoughts and past experiences on to someone. The psychologist went right back through my childhood and upbringing. She also spent a long time talking about sex, with unusual questions like "Does breast feeding turn you on?" Apparently, a lot of your faults can be traced back to your sexual tastes. I didn't really understand that one, apart from when she said I needed to be mothered. I understood that, as I had already thought that Gabby looked a lot like my mother when she was young.

We went through my past couple of sexual encounters with the couples I had met, and she seemed to think I had low self-esteem, and she asked me how I felt immediately after these encounters. I had to admit I did feel quite low afterwards and very guilty. I felt like it was something I should not have done. I only saw the psychologist a few more times. I stopped going as I started to feel a lot better about myself. I did not have a mental illness; I just had to learn to calm my temper down and to acknowledge that violence is not acceptable in a lot of instances, and sex should only be between two people who love each other, and not used as a toy for pleasure. There were far too many emotions involved for that.

On a Saturday not long after, Gabby and I went to see my parents. My father had gone over to the pub that was on the main high street with shops on both sides of the road. We popped down to the shops to get my mother a few things, and as was the normal on a Saturday, the traffic was stopped along the high street. We were crossing the road between the stationary cars when this small open-top sports car beside me sounded the horn very loudly, making me jump.

I was carrying two carrier bags of shopping, and I was wearing a dark-brown checked tweed jacket with two leather elbows. Yes, I know I looked like a teacher or a social worker. I turned and glared at the sports car driver. There were two young Mediterranean-looking blokes in their twenties laughing at me in the car. They were both wearing white T-shirts and looked like they had muscular arms.

I stepped on to the pavement beside an AA shop and the entrance to the local theatre. I handed the bags to Gabby, along with my jacket.

I turned and said to the two idiots, “Get out, you wankers, and I’ll wipe the floor with you.”

They took me up on the challenge and jumped out of the car, then quickly one got behind me and grabbed my arms, whilst the other one started to hit me. I took a couple of punches, then I managed to shake my arms free. I twisted and hit the man behind me, who went straight down to the floor. Then I turned back, and the other bloke had gone between the other cars running away from me.

I shouted, “Come here, you wanker, and fight.”

He came back, and I met him between a car and a lorry, and we exchanged a couple of punches. He went down onto the floor but seemed to bounce back up again in one movement, then he ran away again. I turned back towards the pavement, and his mate had his arms raised in surrender.

There were all the shoppers standing around watching all of this, and now there were several policemen milling about as well. They had several police vans blocking the top of the high street from the main broadway and tube stations, causing a lot of heavy congestion. I went back to Gabby and got my jacket from her and put it back on.

A bloke got out of a car and came over to me and said, “Don’t worry, son, I saw it all. I’m off-duty CID.”

Then a policeman approached me and asked me how it all happened. I told him, and this CID bloke showed him his police ID and said, "I can back all that up. It was two onto one, and they came unstuck."

The policeman said to me, "I'm putting this down as an incident in the street, but if there is any more trouble later, I will nick you."

I thanked him, and I watched as another couple of policemen escorted the two heroes back to their sports car. Our eyes met, and you could see it written all over their face: "Why the fuck did we choose him to pick on?"

My father came up to me and shook my hand, as he had come out of the pub with his mates and watched it all. When we got back up to my parents' flat, I knew I had been in a scrap as I had a banging headache, and I knew I had taken far more punches than I should have. I made sure I never wore that jacket with the leather elbow patches ever again.

That night in the pub, a mate of mine was complaining about being stuck in the traffic near the broadway earlier, and he heard a traffic report on the radio while he was sitting in the traffic saying there was an incident in the street.

I said, "That was me fighting two blokes," and we all laughed.

At this time, I applied to get on the TV show *The Gladiators*. I was invited to audition at the Queen Mother Sports Centre, Victoria. I went along with my training gear in a bag. I was shocked to see the place was packed. We were herded like a load of cattle, being told to go here and there by these people with clipboards. Eventually it was my turn to enter the gym and to get set up on one of six treadmills.

We each had a girl in front of our machine with a stopwatch. We had to complete three miles in a certain time. We all started, and the girl in front of me kept saying, "You need to speed up," and "You are falling behind the clock."

Towards the end, we were all going full pelt on our respective treadmills, when I heard this crash! The big lad on the machine next to me had slipped and gone flying off backwards, crashing into the wall.

I tried to keep going, but the girl said, "Sorry, you are too slow. Please slow your machine to warm down. Thank you for coming."

When I walked out, there was so much merchandise on sale, with the gladiators' pictures all over the place, all very commercial marketing.

Three of my mates decided to invite me along with them to go skiing in the French Alps. It was something I had never done before, and I thought, *Why not? Let's give it a go*. We piled into a jeep that my mate owned, and we drove onto the channel tunnel train, then all the way down through France to this small town high up in the Alps.

My friends had been coming here for a few years and were very competent skiers. Each day I would get up early to go on the baby slopes for my two-hour lesson, and they would get up later. I would then meet them for some breakfast, and we would all go up onto the slopes for the rest of the day and have a good laugh. Usually the best laughs were me falling off the button lifts or losing a ski when falling for the twentieth time. Getting towards the end of our week break, every day we had watched in amazement at this parachutist flying over us in the sky with another skier strapped to him. We kept egging each other on to try it, but we all thought a person had to be mad to go up there.

After a few drinks one afternoon, I volunteered to give it a go on the following day, but only if the others all came up with me to the lift-off point. They all accepted the challenge. The time came when we had to get to the top of the highest mountain over the Alps. None of us had ever been this high before. The chairlift stopped, and then we had to get onto this highest chairlift, which had rarely been used, as the only people who came up this high were the nutters who went off-piste or the parachutist and his prey.

I could not back out now, as there was no other way for me to get back down, as I could not ski the black runs to get down. We were all laughing when my mates realised they had no choice but to ski back down via the black runs that even they would struggle with. I met the parachutist, who seemed a very calm chap. He laid out his parachute in the snow behind us, and then he removed the orange bunting that was preventing people from falling over the edge of the mountain. He called me to ski over to him. He placed me in front of him and hooked me to a seat behind me.

He then said whilst opening his arms out wide, "We now wait for the wind."

I am standing upright with him close behind me breathing on the back of my neck, my mates all pissing themselves laughing at my terrified face. Then he gave me a nudge forwards, and we went over the edge of the mountain. I had never been so scared, skiing down the face of a mountain to certain death, then whoosh! Up we went into the sky.

I sat back into the seat, and I raised my two skis up vertically in front of me. He had sat down with his two knees behind me and either side of my head. We were flying around the mountain tops with my mates very small below. It was amazing, being buffeted by the wind from all sides. I could see the main buildings and the bars where we sat outside looking up at the parachutist – it was a great feeling.

We were up for about an hour, then he shouted, "We are coming down to land."

He told me to stand up as soon as I felt the snow under my skis. We approached this flat, long area of snow, and I felt my skis hit the snow, but as I tried to stand up my legs went to jelly and I rolled along the snow with him behind me and us both getting tangled up in his parachute strings.

When we eventually got free and stood up, he rolled up his parachute and put it into a big rucksack and onto his back. He was not very happy, as he didn't even say goodbye – he just went off in a huff. I now realised he had left me at the third-highest mountain plateau. I hadn't skied down from this height before, but I had to get down and I was still full of adrenaline, so off I went and fell down the first slope and rolled down the next, eventually getting back to our usual bar.

My mates had only just got there as well from skiing all the way down the black runs. We stayed there all day and we all got very drunk. What a great day that was. We got talking to this local lad who owned a bungee-jumping business in the summer. He told us some great stories of having to strap himself to scared ladies, and then jumping with them screaming. He said he had done over a thousand jumps, and he had even done a jump on a BMX bike. He had us all laughing for ages.

Unfortunately, the holiday didn't end well, as we found ourselves in the wrong place at the wrong time. The resort only had a small nightclub, and it was very dark and dingy. This French ski instructor accused one of us of looking at his girlfriend or something silly. An argument took place in the club between us and this instructor. I noticed a couple of French thugs looking on. A couple of my friends walked out, leaving me and the last friend sitting at the bar near to this instructor. One of these French thugs then hit the instructor a few times, knocking him to the floor. Me and my friend immediately left the club.

I thought that was the end of it, but after I finished my ski lesson the next morning, one of the English instructors came to me and told me, "That French ski instructor had to go to hospital last night for an operation on his jaw and cheekbone. Where's your mate, as they think he did it?"

I explained that our friend had already left the club before anything had happened, and it was a French bloke I had not seen before who hit the instructor.

He went on to say, "Well, they think it was an English bloke, and you and your mates are right in the frame for it. The gendarmes are on their way here. The instructor is outside the main building with a gun to shoot your mate. He's from Corsica, and they don't fuck about. They won't kill you, but they will shoot you in the arse, because it is so painful, and it takes a long time to heal."

I ran up to our hotel rooms and woke them all up and explained everything that had happened. Our friend who had drove us said he would go down with me to get the jeep started up, and for the other two to go down the side of the mountain, and we'd drive down and pick them up and then get off home a day earlier than planned.

When the two of us walked down in the main building to get the jeep, there was the French instructor with a bandaged nose and face with two big guys. They saw us and called us over. We were cool about it and explained that we had nothing to do with what had happened to him.

He said, "It was your friend, and I have something here for him," patting his right thigh pocket.

We remonstrated, but they weren't listening. We just walked away, but talk about bad timing, the jeep's battery was dead. The driver went to get a charger. I saw the gendarmes coming up the mountain road in several police cars, and I thought, *fuck it, I've got to get out of here.* I knew if they arrested all of us, and then got a copy of my criminal record from England, they would add two and two together and get three. Don't forget: at that time in France there was no bail for foreign nationals. If you were charged with an offence, you could spend three months in a French prison awaiting trial, even if you were innocent, as we were.

I scurried down the side of the mountain to meet the other two, but they were nowhere to be seen. I started walking with my thumb stuck out for a lift. A van stopped and took me about five miles out of the mountain roads of the Alps, after another couple of lifts I was in a town called Grenoble.

It was then I realised that we had given all our passports to one of our friends at the start of the holiday to look after. I went to an ATM bank machine and withdrew as much money as I could. I then got a train to Lyon, then another train to Paris. It was late at night now and the main train station was empty, so I spread out on two seats and thought I'd have a sleep. Then a policeman came over to me with his fierce-looking dog, telling me the station was closing and I could not stay there.

I walked out into the Parisian streets and the pouring rain. I saw a small building site on a main road. I climbed over the six-foot wooden hoarding. They had a large drum cement mixer that I thought would do to shelter me from the rain if I slept under it, but the ground was soaking wet. There were some bags of cement under a cover, so I got under the cover and slept on the warm bags of cement for a few hours.

When I woke up and climbed back over the hoarding, the rain had ceased, and it was 6:00 a.m. in the morning. I went back into the train station, and I noticed my trousers were white all down one side from the cement. I noticed on the departures board something called a Eurostar train to Waterloo London. I approached the ticket booth and asked what Eurostar was. The lady explained to me it was the channel tunnel train direct to Waterloo Station in London. I asked to purchase a ticket, and she asked for my passport. I explained to her I had everything stolen and I just wanted to get home. I had my subcontractor's 715 exemption certificate card on me, and I showed her this as it had my photo and national insurance number on it. She accepted it and gave me a ticket to Waterloo.

I was starting to feel happier now, thinking I may be able to get home without being arrested by the gendarmes, but to my horror I saw a queue of people heading for my train and two gendarmes checking their passports as they filtered through the gates to the train. My mind was in fugitive mode now, and I felt like I was in a movie. I noticed this woman on her own with three small children, and she was holding her several passports out, spread like a fan. I jostled through the queue past a couple of people who were shouting and pulling at me, but nothing was going to stop me getting tight to this woman. I stuck to her from behind, and by the time she turned around, I had pushed her through past the two gendarmes, leaving them to think I was with her.

I then got onto the train into the first carriage I came to, and I sat down beside the window. A young lady sat down beside me. I smiled as I thought I was almost home now. I thought about my friends back at the ski resort high in the Alps, and I hoped they had got away before the gendarmes got them. The train was going quite fast, and I was happy, but then it stopped at a small station just before entering the tunnel. A lady train official came through the train asking to see passports. Your mind plays tricks on you, and my paranoia set in. Had the gendarmes in the ski resort sent through my details as a wanted person to all ports and airports? The lady official asked to see my passport. I explained how I had everything stolen and the gendarmes had put me onto the train. Because it was a bank holiday weekend with all the embassies shut, they told me to go back to England, and I would go to the Irish embassy when it opened to report my passport being stolen. I then gave her my 715 card and said they told me it was okay to get back home with this.

She went away for ages, then came back and returned the card, saying it was fine. Now at last I thought I was finally getting home, but there was still one more hurdle to get over. As we walked off the train in Waterloo Station, there was a new customs section. This was all new to me, as the last time I was in Waterloo Station as a kid it was just a train station – now it was more like an airport with a green 'nothing to declare' section. As I walked through, this young official stopped me. I thought, *At least I got a long way before they caught me,* but he started on saying, "You do know, sir, it is illegal to bring drugs into the country."

I could have kissed him. He made me take off my Caterpillar boots, and he gave them to someone to go and X-ray them. He made me turn out my pockets, and he asked me all about where I had been. I told him I only got as far as Paris before I got robbed of my passport. I then realised in my things were ATM receipts from banks in Grenoble, Lyon, and Paris, and I looked like a panda – all brown from the Alps sun, with white circles around my eyes from the ski goggles. Lucky for me he wasn't really interested, and he was just making small talk until my boots returned. The boots came back all clear, and he said, "Off you go." I got onto a tube train and thought, *Finally I am now home.*

When I got to Gabby's place, she was overjoyed to see me. One of my friends had called her from France saying they didn't know where I was, and that I may have been shot by the French instructor, or fallen down the mountain side in the snow and froze to death. Not very subtle, my friends. It was Saturday midday, and Gabby was just going out to the launderette to wash some clothes. I stripped off naked and gave her all of mine, as I had been travelling in them for two days. I went to bed in the quiet flat, and after a couple of hours, I was woken up by the phone ringing. I picked it up and I heard, "Roger, is that you?"

It was one of my friends, and they were still in France. He was phoning to see if Gabby had heard anything from me. He told me I had done them a favour, because the gendarmes had picked the two of them up down the mountain somewhere, and then they got the third one when he tried to leave in the jeep. They had kept them in the police station all night trying to get them to admit it was me who had hit the French ski instructor. They were banging the table saying, "We know it was your friend, Roger the boxer. He cannot get away. We have his passport."

That did make me laugh. We met in the pub the next day, Sunday morning, and they gave me back all my belongings that had been in the jeep – and my passport. They told me how they were let out midmorning without charge. The gendarmes dropped them back to the resort, then waited in a police car out of sight. When they had got all their things and left the resort, they were followed by the police car sitting about four cars back from them. The gendarmes thought they were going to pick me up somewhere along the way, as they had given them all the passports back, including mine. What the gendarmes didn't realise was that 'Roger the boxer' was already back in good old blighty.

In the pub that Sunday, it was a double celebration, as another friend of ours was back from prison on a weekend home leave. He thought our whole story was amazing, and he said he couldn't wait to tell the lads back inside. I returned to France some years later for a golfing break, and there were no issues or problems with my passport being checked, and everyone in France was very friendly to me. Maybe they caught the guilty party after we left the ski resort, but I'm glad I didn't hang about and take a chance on them believing us that we had nothing to do with what had happened.

Chapter Nine
Moving On

I phoned up an advert in the London evening paper that read, *Bricklayers and Supervisors wanted.* I went over to an office in East London to meet the subcontractors. There were two of them, and they seemed like two good blokes with no messing. I started on a site for them just as a bricklayer to start with, then they said they would promote me to a foreman if they thought I was good enough. After a few weeks, they asked me if I would live and work away from home, as they had a site in the West Country starting in a week's time. I said, "Yes, sure, I'd be up for that."

Gabby was fine with me working away all week and coming home at the weekends. We weren't getting on that great anyway at the time; she was having trouble with her stomach and now pregnant, and I was my usual idiot self with little sympathy. I started this large construction site in the West Country with four other men from London who had worked for these subcontractors for many years, and they all knew each other very well. I had to get to know them and to fit in somehow. They had rented a large house for us to share whilst there from Monday to Friday each week. The first night we went out to a local pub, and we were sitting enjoying a nice quiet drink when behind us there was this awful racket and a smashing sound. We thought it had all kicked off and there must be a big fight starting. When we looked in the next bar, they were throwing wooden balls down an alley, knocking over wooden skittles. It was their local pub sport. We all laughed and enjoyed watching all these locals with funny accents enjoying themselves.

This was a large project, and we would be away from home for some time. I had already met an ex-boxer who told me where to go for some training and sparring. He was a very experienced boxer at both amateur and professional levels. We went on to have some great sparring sessions, and he was a lot of fun.

After a month or so, I met this very attractive girl. I say *girl* rather than *woman*, as she was a lot younger than me. I felt guilty about being unfaithful to Gabby, but I was a typical bloke who followed his penis rather than any brain cells.

Gabby moved back to her parents' house. I was at work in my site office one day when I took a phone call from my wife's best friend, who told me I was the father of a baby boy born that morning. He had come a bit early, and they were both being kept in hospital as a precaution. A few days later, I drove up to the hospital to see Gabby and the new arrival, Daniel. I held him and he was tiny. It was nice to see Gabby and the baby. I felt terrible for what I had put her through. I had been very selfish.

Two months later, the West Country girl told me she was pregnant. We decided to get married. That's when everything changed after we got married. We were just not getting on, and I realised then we had both made a terrible mistake. I packed everything into a van I had borrowed from a mate, and we drove back to her parents' house. I told them it was all over. I had been such an idiot, and quite rightly I blamed myself for everything. I was the older person, and I should have known better. It was clear she no longer wanted me, but we had to wait for twelve months before we could get legally divorced.

The divorce went through without any objections, and I didn't hear from her again until the child was sixteen years old and wanted to meet me. We met in the West Country over a coffee, and I had to explain that I could not disrupt both of our lives after hearing nothing for sixteen years. We both accepted that, and we parted amicably.

I continued to build the project, and each weekend my boxing mate from there would come up to London, and I'd take him to a pro gym for sparring with some professional boxers. Whilst back in London, I got in touch with Gabby and little Daniel, who was three months old now. With her being a single parent, they had moved into a large council house temporarily, while the council found a permanent flat for them. We were getting on well, and I looked after the baby a couple of times while Gabby went out with some friends. I made sure I went to see them every time I was back in London at the weekends.

I had finished the large original project in the West Country and moved on to an even larger site. Whilst working away I had sold my flat and bought a small terrace house just up the road. After a few months, Gabby and Daniel moved in with me permanently. I carried on with the project, looking after over one hundred men once again. It was the largest building project in the UK at the time.

I looked forward to returning to London each weekend and seeing little Daniel with Gabby. I had a rented house provided by my employers, and everything was ticking along just fine.

I had returned to play rugby every Saturday. We came up against London Scottish fourth team, and they were way ahead of us with fitness and skill levels. Their hooker was only about five feet two inches tall but as wide as a house. In the scrums, I just couldn't get down low enough, and he kept lifting me, and my neck was twisting in the process. By the second half, I was getting spasms down my neck and into my shoulders. The game ended with them winning by fifty points to our three points. Back in the clubhouse, we had a few drinks and something to eat (always chilli con carne).

When I woke on Sunday morning, I couldn't move my head, and my neck ached with the spasms that had returned. I phoned a back specialist that I knew, and he asked me to come to his surgery right away. Whilst there, he examined me and did some things to my neck, spine, and shoulders. He then told me, "You have a ruptured vertebra, and the difference between a ruptured vertebra and a broken vertebra is luck. You could have been paralysed from the neck down if it hadn't been for your strong neck. You have ripped soft tissue going under your shoulder that will take a few months at least to heal. No more rugby for you, I'm afraid."

After I left his surgery and in the next couple of days, the spasms stopped, and the pain relented quite a bit. I could move and turn my head, but only in a restricted way. I did play rugby the following Saturday and still in the front row, but on the outside of the scrum as a prop forward. I just couldn't get the hang of it, though, with all the pressure just on one side of my body, and I was also very worried about my neck. That was me finished with rugby, although a top rugby player who played for a premier league team – there was no professionalism in rugby union then – was working on our site as a manager for the main contractors. He arranged a charity sevens tournament that I played in, but it wasn't serious and it was just a good laugh with no real physical scrums or bad tackles.

Whilst on this large project, I went to the bank one day and I noticed the bank had made a mistake. They had put £2,000 into my account. I didn't touch it, and that weekend I asked a friend's wife who worked for this bank what I should do.

She replied, "It's their mistake. Go and spend it."

On the Monday I went to the bank and withdrew the money. I went to a travel agent and booked a holiday for me and my son James to Disney World in Florida in a few weeks. We had a great time, although it didn't start very well. When we got off the plane and approached passport control, I showed the man my Irish passport, which also had my son on it. He said, "Could you move to the side and wait there, please?" Then a different man came over with a policeman who had a gun, and they took us to a little office.

I had no idea what was going on. We sat there for about an hour, and I was trying to reassure James that it was just a security check or something, and that we'd soon be at our hotel enjoying ourselves. They came into the office with a representative of the airline, who started to grill me about 'how did I manage to get on to the plane and then off it again without a proper visa'. Apparently, they had changed the law recently, and with an Irish passport you had to have a visa now.

It was news to me, and I said, "I did everything right, the travel agent said I did not need a visa, and your staff inspected my passport when I was getting on and also when I was getting off. When the plane was coming down to land, they came through the plane's cabin asking if anyone needed a visa form, and I asked if I needed one with an Irish passport, and the stewardess said no."

He wasn't very happy with his staff, as the airline would now get a $10,000 fine for allowing me to get off the plane. I also had to pay a $300 fine – that took a lump out of my spending money for the holiday. By the time they let us out and it was all sorted, everyone in the terminal had gone. The place was empty with all the carousels stopped, apart from one that was going around and around with just the one case on it, which was mine. Then this lady travel rep came up to us and asked my name. She apologised for all the goings on, then said to go with her to a private car that would take us to the hotel. Then we had a good time. Disney World was amazing, with rides like Space Mountain and then the scary Twilight Zone Tower of Terror, where you fell thirteen floors in an elevator car. We also went to SeaWorld, where the whales and dolphins were great.

We went out at midnight one night on an excursion from the hotel to take a ride on an airboat that skimmed across the shallow waters of the everglades to see alligators. It wasn't dark at first, and you could see the rocket launching site of Cape Canaveral in the distance. Everyone sat at the back on the boat beside the large propeller. My son and I sat right at the front, thinking they were all mugs or scared. When we started scooting across the water on the everglades –

and it had got dark now – my son and I were pelted by a million flies hitting us right in the face. That's why they were sitting at the back. Who were the mugs?

We returned home after having a great time to several letters from the bank wanting their money back. I strung them along for twelve months but eventually paid them it back. I complained to the travel agents about the mishap with the visa, and they gave me £500 in compensation.

I slipped up, though, as my mate's wife who worked for the bank told me later: "You should have asked for a holiday for two anywhere in the world, and they would probably have given it to you."

Never mind, I was happy with the money.

After finishing the large project, I went to build a new hospital. I was given a rented house a mile or so down the road and just into the main town. This was a large project but not as big as the previous one. I had about seventy men on it, but it was a difficult area to get bricklayers, and we had to advertise all along the South Coast to find them. I found the local boxing club, and they were pleased for me to help with some of the training and to spar with their best boxers. I had a couple of mates with me from London, which helped as they were good bricklayers and I could trust them not to take any nonsense from the men.

As always with me, trouble wasn't far away, and I got to know the names of the faces in that area. One of the bricklayers was well connected to one of the main men, who owned a pub near the town centre. He offered to introduce me to him. I went with him to this pub one evening with one of my London pals. This pub landlord was a big fella, and we got on well. He said he had a friend doing life in Dartmoor Prison. I thought, *Well, he must be nearing the end of his time*, as Dartmoor was only a cat-C prison, and not for lifers.

Later that evening after everyone had gone, he said, "I've got someone I want you to meet," and he introduced me to a bloke who had just come into the pub.

We shook hands, and he sat down to join us at the table. He immediately started questioning me about boxing and who I had fought.

Then he said, "I've got a fighter who will fight you for £1,000 here in the pub. He's a middleweight coloured kid from South London, and he's had two hundred fights. We can put a rope from the pool table over to the bar and back across to the far wall, for you to box in. We'll put the £1,000 cash from each of you on the bar, and the last man standing can take the £2,000 cash. The guvnor can run the book for the betting. What do you say?"

I just laughed out loud. "What is this boxer's name?"

A coloured kid from South London who has had two hundred fights? I would know him. He paused for a bit too long, then came up with Leroy something.

I turned to the pub governor and said, "Is this a wind-up?"

He replied, "You see that cunt there? He's the biggest grass you could meet, and he got a lot of people put away last year."

I now had no choice, and I hit this spoof boxing manager with a straight right, and I followed it up with the usual combinations and plenty of kicks to keep him on the floor.

I turned to the governor and said, "You satisfied now?" then I walked out of the pub with my mate.

The whole thing had been a set up to test my credentials. I was angry afterwards, but then I calmed down and I accepted it was the circles I moved in that were to blame. It did me no harm, because when the word went around the site in the following days, all the South Coast men now knew to keep their heads down and to get the bricks laid. I never went back to that pub, and I just continued to help at the boxing club – that was enough for me.

We had a large Irish contractor doing the concrete frame of the building. They had about two hundred men on the site, many of them living away from home like us. We were having a good drink with them one night in a local pub. I naturally got on well with them due to telling them about my father in the tunnels and being Irish. We were all getting drunk as the night was coming to an end when these two big Irish lads had a falling-out and started to fight. My natural instincts kicked in, and I jumped up and got between the two of them, with one hand on their chests to hold them back. This was not a good move, as I was now getting hit on either side of my face and head by each of their punches in turn.

It quietened down, and we all went home to bed. The next day on the site, we all laughed along with these Irish lads, who thought it was hysterical that I had taken most of the punches. I had to laugh, but I still had a headache. We finished the project and left behind a fantastic new hospital. In 1996 I was invited by Gabby's dad to go with him in the early hours of the morning to his brother's house in Stamford Hill, North London, which was a predominantly Jewish area. His brother had a large-screen TV, and we were going to watch the boxing match between Frank Bruno and Mike Tyson, live from Las Vegas.

I should tell you Gabby's uncle was George Harrison Marks, the famous photographer from the 1950s, '60s, and '70s who specialised in very artistic sex pictures and films. His most famous film was *Come Play with Me* starring Mary Millington. He was a fantastic character to meet. He told me he was born in this house and he used to play out on the street when he was a kid during the war, with Mike and Bernie Winters, the renowned double act from TV fame. The house was like an Aladdin's cave, with the walls covered with expensive things hanging up. He had George Formby's original ukulele and Napoleon's war mask – unbelievable. He told me all about his work and studios, and he laughed when he told me, "I've been a millionaire three times, married three times, and bankrupt three times."

In 1997 I proposed to Gabby. We had known each other since 1991, and it seemed like the right thing to do. We got married in the local registry office, with all our family there, one week before Christmas. My best man was an old pal. Some of my old school mates turned up, and quite a few from Paddington as well, which was fantastic, and I was very happy to see them all. They were all proper friends. I was a lucky fellow. Gabby, Daniel, and I went to Edinburgh for a few days' honeymoon. We had a great time, and Daniel enjoyed seeing all the animals in the large zoo there. It was nice to be working from home once again with Gabby and Daniel nearby.

In 1997 we heard the sad news that her Uncle George had died. I told Gabby to go to the funeral with her dad, and I would look after Daniel. Her Uncle George was such a character that he had written his own script for his funeral to be followed on the day, and they all ended up back at the Old Bull and Bush pub in Hampstead for a good old drink.

I started a project in Henley-on-Thames. It was a fantastic project to be involved in, due to the smaller-than-usual handmade red bricks. The architects had designed a wonderful complex of several buildings in an inner square with large flat arches over large openings. I had a great bricklayer there as my No. 2; he was a real character and from a family who were from North London, with all the boys being bricklayers just like their father had been. He was leaving early one Friday, as he was taking his wife away for a romantic weekend in a posh hotel.

When I got back to my office at about 4:00 p.m. from a site meeting, he had left a funny note on my desk, "See you on Monday," and a smiley face. I went home thinking, *I hope he has a great weekend as he deserves it.* I couldn't have done the job without him. When I got to my office early on Monday, at 7:00 a.m., I sat down to drink my early cup of tea and the phone rang. It was my No.

2's wife, who told me he had died on Friday night of a heart attack. He was only forty-two years old. I was staring at his coat hanging in the corner with his boots underneath and his hard hat. What a shock. I wasn't sure whether we should all go home for the day.

As the men came into sign-in, I told them the sad news. I gathered them all together and asked them what they would like to do. They were all unanimous to stay and get on with the work, as that was what he would have wanted them to do. I said okay, and we all just got on with it, but I can honestly say it was the longest day of my life. I couldn't wait to get home and have a good cry. I finished the project and then moved on to a smaller project in 1998.

Chapter Ten
Prison Life

On the new project, as always, I had a couple of my London friends on the site, and we all had a good laugh on most days whilst at work. I had already been on the site for one week, and on this following Monday I had six new men starting to get the job started properly. On this project there was a site manager called Rodney, and he was only about five feet tall, which was quite unusual in the construction industry. As I took the six new men from the car park to the site offices, I said, "You will all first have to do a site induction with Big Rod, but it will only take about thirty minutes."

One of the lads said, "Why is he called Big Rod?"

I replied, "Because he is probably the biggest man you have ever seen. He's about six feet eight inches tall and as wide as a house."

You can imagine what happened when they were all sitting there, waiting for the site induction to start, and 'Big Rod' walked in at only five feet tall. They all instinctively fell about laughing; they just couldn`t stop. Until Rod, to his credit said, "Well, now we've got all the childish humour out of the way, let's get this induction started, shall we?"

After it was completed, I had a quiet word with Rod, and I apologised, explaining how it was all my fault and I should have realised what would happen. He was very good about it and said it happens quite often and didn't bother him.

Then he smiled and said, "Just remember it's me that has to agree to your dayworks and any extras on the job."

We shook hands and parted, both smiling.

One Friday we finished as usual, but as I went into the main contractor's office this arrogant young manager who was still wet behind the ears from his university days pulled me aside and said, "I hope you're going to cover all those blocks up."

He was referring to two lorry loads of blocks we had just unloaded at the far end of the site. All of my men had now left the site, so I said, "They'll be okay until Monday as the forecast is dry and sunny all weekend."

But he was adamant they had to be covered, or he would do it and charge us for doing it. I really hated young managers with no common sense, who thought because they had been given a tiny position of responsibility, they were going to change the world all by themselves, with their head stuck firmly up their own arse. I stormed out and went to the blocks with a couple of rolls of polythene, and after about thirty minutes they were all covered. I got into my car and drove away with the tyres screaming – I was not happy. I drove along the dual carriage way to a large roundabout nearby that usually had traffic lights to control each road as it met the roundabout, so traffic from one road could enter the roundabout whilst the other roads were stationary at the red lights. It was a very busy roundabout, and this was the Friday rush hour with me in a very bad mood. Our lights changed, and I entered onto the curve of the roundabout, which was moving well in front of me. This big red bus came from nowhere and entered the roundabout from the left. He had to have gone through the red lights. I had to swerve my car up onto the grass in the middle of the roundabout to avoid colliding with the bus. The driver was staring at me and laughing. Another car driver to my side looked at me and shook his head at the bus driver saying, "What is that all about?"

I got back on with driving around the roundabout, and I do not know why, but I went past my exit and back towards the way I came, following the bus. He pulled into a bus stop on the left and I pulled my car in front of the bus across the front to prevent him from moving. People had got off the bus, and I got onto the front platform beside the driver, who was sitting behind a small door up to his waist.

I shouted at the driver, "What the fuck were you doing, putting me up on to the roundabout, you wanker?"

He stood up and told me to fuck off. My fists were going through the air before I even knew it – bang, bang, bang – then I grabbed him by his collar and lifted him over the door and down the steps of the bus, where I hit him again. These two men came running over and pulled me off. I looked around me, and several cars were now stopped and there were a few drivers who were out of their vehicles and talking on their mobile phones, and some were even taking pictures.

I heard someone shout, “Quick! Stop him! He’s getting away,” but there was no one brave enough, and I just got back into my car and I sped off. When I finally got back to my house, I had my dinner and a shower, then I told Gabby what had happened. I went up to my local police station once again and I handed myself in, explaining to the duty sergeant that I’d been involved in a driving incident. I waited in a holding cell until the CID arrived, and they took me back to their base for questioning. They kept me in for most of the night, then charged me with GBH and kicked me out at about 4:00 a.m.

I said, “No lift home then?”

They said, “Fuck off.”

I got a taxi from a local twenty-four-hour mini-cab firm. A month later I was in the local magistrate’s court. My brief managed to get the charge dropped from GBH to ABH. I thought they were going to give me a suspended sentence because of Gabby’s Crohn’s disease, but the magistrate explained to me how serious it was because it involved a public servant, and some of the passenger witnesses had said they were now too scared to catch a bus ever again. He did condemn the bus driver, though, who he said acted totally inappropriately for a public servant in this situation. Before he announced the sentence, I heard the door behind me unlock and I heard the jangle of handcuffs. I knew then I was going down.

He sentenced me to three months in prison, and then he said the words you do not want to hear: “Take him down.”

I was led away and down the stairs to the holding cells. My brief came down and apologised for me receiving a custodial sentence, but he said, “They are having a bit of a purge on violent crime at the moment.”

I was allowed one phone call, so I called Gabby with the bad news. I told her where my car was parked in the multi-storey car park next to the court building on the second floor, and there was a spare car key in the kitchen drawer. Give it to her brother or father to come and get the car and park it outside our house. My bosses could come and collect it if they needed it for someone else whilst I was away. I told Gabby to call my bosses to explain what had happened. I told her not to worry about me as I could handle myself, and it was only three months, which meant with good behaviour I’d be home in six or seven weeks. What I didn’t tell her was my biggest fear that I may never get out ever again. I had learnt a lot about prison life seeing as I was surrounded by people who were in and out all the time, and I had visited quite a few of my friends whilst they were inside. I was scared I would not be able to control my temper, especially if I were to be confronted by an arsehole of a burglar or a paedophile.

I was still shocked that my past bad days and lucky escapes from a prison sentence had finally caught up with me. It seemed I had used up my nine lives, with luck now deserting me. I had no complaints – you can't run around like a lunatic fighting all the time without one day getting a proper collar from the law. There was only one person to blame, and he was sitting right here. When going to court, if you thought you were going to be put in prison, you would bring certain things with you to court that were difficult to get when you were away in prison, like a few hundred pounds cash in your pocket to go into your prison bank account, for you to use whilst you were in there. On one day each week, the inmates queue up to what you could describe as a tuck shop. You give your prison number to the screw behind the counter, and he or she will tell you how much you have in your prison bank account. You can then spend up to £10 of it each week, on items like magazines, books, and a range of groceries and sweets. A good, thick book is always handy, and cigarettes to trade with, as I was a non-smoker, and maybe a good puzzle book, or phone cards, but unfortunately, I was caught by surprise on this day, and I had little with me when I entered the court building. I only had a few quid in my pocket.

They led me by the handcuffs out through the back of the courthouse and up the steps into the sweatbox – the prison transport vehicle. I am naturally quite claustrophobic, and I wasn't looking forward to this, but when I sat down in the cubicle, they took the cuffs off me then locked the door. I noticed the window looking out on the side of the lorry, and another small window where they could look in through my door. It wasn't too bad. The engines started, and off we went out onto the road. I had seen these lorries lots of times on the road with their small blacked-out windows, so I knew the people outside could not see me, but I could see them. We drove for about ninety minutes, then pulled into HMP Woodhill, Milton Keynes. This was a double-A-cat prison. The rumours I had heard was, there were more prison guards and dogs than inmates. There were four of us in the lorry. They now walked us into the prison, all of us now back in handcuffs, then put us all into a holding cell with another five or six new inmates, waiting to be processed and taken to our cells. It was now quite late. A trolley arrived, and they gave each of us a tray with a dinner on it under a silver cover. I had been expecting a kick in the nuts, not a dinner. We got paired up and put into cells in B Wing. This was the wing that housed inmates held on remand whilst their trials were progressing, new arrivals and inmates on induction for their first week, and other inmates doing their time for offences like drinking and driving, burglary, shoplifting, drugs, and low-level violence (like me). I got put into a cell with a Scottish bloke; we got on okay. He got a three-year sentence for drug dealing, and after talking with him I learnt he had spent most of his life going in and out of prison. I thought, *You, my son, will come in very handy for me, to teach me the ropes of the prison regime.*

I knew he was an experienced con as soon as we walked into the cell, as he grabbed the bottom bunk bed straight away, and said, “You’re on top.” This meant I had to climb up to the top bunk bed all the time, and when I got up in the night to use the toilet I’d have to climb down and then back up again.

Our first morning after breakfast we were paraded one by one into a senior officer’s office, where he explained all we needed to know about the prison rules. He informed us the first week was our induction week, and we were not allowed to mix with the other prisoners until our second week. We would be on twenty-three-hour lockup and only allowed out once a day for an hour of recreation in the outside yard. For all meals, we would be allowed out of our cells, escorted to the prison canteen, and permitted to take our meal on a tray back to our cells, where the door would then be locked.

After a couple of days, I was getting used to this process. I couldn’t believe my pad mate. When it was close to our one hour of recreation, I would be hovering around the door like an excited puppy waiting to be let out into the garden. When the screw opened the door, I was out like a shot and walking with the other inmates to the outside yard, but my pad mate stayed on the bed and told the screw to fuck off and shut the door behind him. I couldn’t believe it, but it was his little thing not to give them any power over him. He would just turn over and go back to sleep. It was the same when we returned with our meals. Once we were both in the cell, he would slam the door shut before the screw had time to close it. “I’ll shut my own fucking door,” he’d say.

To get through the twenty-three hours, I used to tell him jokes; he laughed at some of them, but others he’d just tut at. I could open our cell window, which was quite long and narrow, to about two inches; that was enough to breathe in the outside air. I would see a screw walking with a dog, inspecting the inside of the prison outer high wall. I could time him and see him each time he got back to within my eyesight distance. I could see over the wall, but there were only trees to see, and birds flying freely, which was nice.

On one of the days a screw opened my cell door and gave me a couple of letters. One from Gabby, and one from my son James in Northern Ireland. What a great surprise. I sat and read them over and over with tears in my eyes.

James, who was sixteen and still at school, said, "I don't care what you have done. You will always be my dad, and I love you."

That was so nice of him to say something like that. I was overjoyed but also very aware of just how stupid I had been to be in here. The next day when out of the cell getting lunch, I noticed an inmate I recognised. He came from a well-known family in North London; I think he was on remand whilst his case continued at the old bailey.

A couple of the convicts who worked in the kitchen were good blokes, and they would give you a good book to read and newspapers, as they knew you were on twenty-three-hour lockup. It didn't matter if the newspapers were several days old, you still read every single word printed.

One day they moved us to different cells up on the next floor, and we were given new pad mates. I don't know why. I was on the top bunk bed yet again. My new pad mate was a big lump of about six feet and a bit docile and quiet.

He told me right off. "I am a paranoid schizophrenic will that bother you."

I said, "Are you on medication?" and he nodded. I then said, "Well, as long as you take your pills, I'll be fine."

He just nodded. He was in for shoplifting with dodgy credit cards. He worked for someone who used to give him shopping lists of what to buy with dodgy credit cards. He would take all the risks, then hand over the stuff and get a few quid for his troubles. He got caught because he went into a large store and bought something, and then like an idiot he went back into the same store an hour later and bought something else from the same woman behind the counter, but with a completely different credit card. She told him to wait there while she got on the phone. He panicked, jumped over the counter, smashed the phone into her face a few times, took the credit card back, and ran out of the store. The store security staff chased him and pinned him to the floor. He didn't grass up the bloke he worked for, either. I told him when he got out that bloke owed him big time. He just nodded.

I was learning the way of the prison system fast, and when Sunday came along, I was suddenly very religious, as that meant you were allowed out of your cell to go to the chapel. As I walked away from B wing towards the chapel along the path, there was a screw with a dog every two metres. These dogs were huge

German shepherds and barking like mad with screws holding them back. I like dogs, and I wanted to pat one of them on the head, but the screw said, "Come any closer and he'll have your hand off."

I didn't get any closer.

At this time in HMP Woodhill, there were some notorious inmates being held in the double-A-cat block. One most notably had changed his name to that of a famous film star. One day as I was walking towards the outside area, I noticed a screw was just taking off the full riot gear and sweating. He told me he had just come from the double-A-cat block and, along with five other screws, had just taken the notorious inmate out for his one hour of daily exercise. He told me when he got into the small yard, he ran like crazy, around and around the yard, and climbed up the mesh fencing and jumped about all over the place until he was completely tired out. They then dragged him back in and threw him back into his cell. He was kept in solitary confinement as he was a danger to other prisoners. I doubted they would ever let him out. How sad is that for all concerned?

After we completed our induction week, we were allocated jobs for £10 a week. I was allocated a nice easy job called Outside Gardens. This was a very coveted job, as it meant you were escorted outside of the prison through the gates to the car parks every day, and you looked after all the outside flowers, gardens, and fences. What they forgot to mention to me, though, was that every time you went out or into the prison, you would have to have a full body search, and that meant your anus as well.

It was strange being on the outside. You got to see all the visitors queueing up at the side door of the prison. There was this large van parked near to us, and one of the other inmates said to me, "See that blond bird kissing the driver of that van? She is visiting her husband, who is a lifer. I bet she doesn't tell him about the bloke in the van." I just laughed.

The work was quite physical, but it was only a few hours each day, and we had a full hour lunch break included in a secure shed, with sandwiches laid out for us and tea or coffee. The main screw supervising us loved chess, and each day he would take us on to challenge him. I loved chess, but he was too good even for me. We would get approached by other inmates who wanted us to pick up a packet for them dropped outside and stick it up our arse or swallow it, then shit it out and give it to them. I always said no, as my arse was sacred to me and I didn't want it to end up looking like the Blackwall Tunnel, thank you.

I met lots of different inmates – plenty of burglars, who I despised. To me and the way I was brought up, these burglars were scumbags. They would soon get the message I wanted nothing to do with them. I met a couple of older businesspeople, who had defrauded the HMRC or VAT people, usually with imports or exports not being declared, or they'd created false companies to steal all the VAT, then shut them down and scarpered. A bit like the old days when villains would play the *Long Firm* game. That's when you could rent a building with a false identity and set up a company using false details. Then fill the place up with goods to sell that you have purchased yourself with cash. After a couple of months, the suppliers would give you credit to purchase more goods from them. When you got to the maximum of your credit allowed, you would then sell all of the goods and shut the company down over a weekend. On the Monday there would be an empty building, and you would have disappeared.

The saddest inmates were the drink drivers. I met one inmate who had lost everything. He was stopped for erratic driving in his car and was found to be four times over the limit. He was sentenced to six weeks in prison. He then lost his job and his wife, who had walked out on him, and his house was being repossessed. He was not very happy, even with only three weeks to do. Whereas I had just spoken to Gabby on the phone, who told me that my bosses had collected the car, and they gave her a lump sum cheque to cover my six weeks' wages whilst I was away from work. How about that for good bosses, and what I would call proper good people?

I would wind the screws up by telling them, "I'm getting £800 a week for being in here. How much are you earning each week?"

They would reply, "But I get to go home each night to my house and my family."

Ouch. Touché!

The next day was our visitor's day, and Gabby and one of my bosses came to see me, which was great. Gabby was all smiles as usual and turned a few heads as she walked in; it was nice to smell the perfume and steal a kiss. A week later, my father and my brother Steve came to see me. I felt bad they had to go through all the rigmarole of such tight security at Woodhill. They took the visitors' fingerprints to make sure visitors didn't swap places with the inmate they were visiting, but my father had no fingerprints. His fingers were smooth and flat with no prints due to his age and all the hard work he'd done over his lifetime. They let him in anyway. I suppose they realised that I had fingerprints, so we could hardly swap places. It was fantastic to see them both, and it really cheered me up. I felt myself getting ten times stronger just by seeing my father and brother. I think it settled them as well, to know I was doing fine and handling myself well in the circumstances.

After a couple of weeks in Woodhill, I was told I was getting categorised as a cat-D prisoner and shipped out early the next morning to an open prison called North Sea Camp, Boston, Lincolnshire. I didn't sleep very well that night as I was excited to be getting away from Woodhill. They opened my door up at 5:00 a.m. and took me to the sweatbox lorry waiting at the gate. It was a long drive all the way to Lincolnshire from Milton Keynes, but luckily, they had to stop at a prison near Newmarket called HMP Highpoint to pick up another inmate. They got us out and into the prison canteen for some lunch, then back into the sweatbox. There was a women's section at Highpoint that held the famous inmate Myra Hindley.

We arrived at HMP North Sea Camp quite late that day. It had taken over four hours to get there. I was just glad to get out of the sweatbox. It was weird, as when we got out of the lorry, there were lots of inmates all lined up watching us, and it reminded me of the film *The Shawshank Redemption*. We were each given a lecture on the prison and then shown to our cells. I say cells, but it was really a large room. The prison used to be an RAF camp during WWII, and it looked like the prison of war huts you'd see in the old war films on TV, all low level, wooden, and very long. I had to share with a young Indian lad. It was quite a large room with single beds placed against opposite walls. I was glad not to have to climb up onto a top bunk bed finally. There were two tables between the beds and a one-metre square window above the tables. There was no toilet, though, but here was the best bit: as a cat-D open prisoner you got your own door key. Yes, you could go out to use the toilet at the end of the corridor with the shower rooms, whenever you pleased.

A couple of inmates who had been in there for a while told me not to take a job cutting the cabbages or in with the pigs, as you stank all the time, which wasn't very nice. The prison had its own farm growing cabbages and potatoes, spread out over hundreds of acres. It also bred pigs. The following morning, I was in front of the prison job allocation officer, who asked me if I had any limitations to what sort of job I could do.

I replied, "Yes, sir. As a bricklayer, I have always struggled with a bad back, and I cannot bend up and down very much. I also have a fear of animals, sir."

He looked at me and smiled, then said, "Okay, you can be the new toilet and showers cleaner, then."

I was very happy with that. The toilets and showers were all stainless steel, no glass mirrors for obvious reasons, just shiny stainless steel you could see your face in. All the walls and floors were tiled, and there was a drain gulley running down the centre of the floor. This made cleaning them a doddle. After all the inmates had gone off to do their work on the farm and elsewhere, I would squirt Jif cleaner all over the walls and floor, then wipe the surfaces clean and hose the floor and walls down, then mop everything to the floor gulley and away.

Quite often there would be an empty bottle of Jack Daniels or vodka in the bin, so I would discreetly take the rubbish out to the large collection of bins at the front of the block, not letting the screws see the empties, or there would be an enquiry and they'd want to know how someone got the booze into the prison. I knew, as I had seen an inmate one night arriving back after running across the one hundred acres of farmland with a few bottles in a bag that a mate had dropped off.

This was a great job, although I would have to clean morning, after lunch, and late in the evening, but I had mastered the whole process, and it would only take me about twenty minutes each time. In the mornings, after I had cleaned the toilets and showers, I could go to the main screw's office and collect my daily newspaper to read. We got £10 a week in wages, but I had Gabby send in some more money to put into my account with the prison service. I could pay for newspapers for the whole week in advance, and they would be delivered every day. It was up to the screws whether they let you have them or not, but I was no trouble to them, and I got on okay with everyone, as I knew it was the only way I would ever get out.

Believe me, there were a few times I had to hold back from hitting one of the idiots in there. At times it was like living in the very worst council estate imaginable, with the worst neighbours from hell all around you, and you were not allowed to lose your temper. It was tough on the day of little Daniel's fifth birthday. I phoned Gabby, and she told me she had bought Daniel a little drum kit, and her dad had wrapped it all up and put it in the porch outside our front door. When they got up in the morning and Daniel was all excited about it being his birthday, Gabby, who had been telling him I was working away for a couple of months, said, "Let's look outside the door to see if Daddy has sent you anything." Then she described his face and the excitement of it all. I was crying on the other end of the phone with tears running down my face – tears of joy but also of sadness at not being there. How stupid was I. I was so grateful to Gabby and her father.

A big help to me was the prison gymnasium. I was telling the officer looking after it about my boxing, and he was a big fan of boxing. There were several punch bags hanging up at the end of the gym. He told me if I went to see the main prison governor and asked politely, he could allow me to have my skipping rope sent in, as long as it was kept in the gym office under lock and key whenever I wasn't using it. He said he would back me up to have it, as it was necessary for my boxing training. A week later, Gabby had sent in my old faithful skipping rope. I'll always remember the gym officer and the other inmates' faces when I first got going with the rope. I was jumping twice in the air whilst spinning the rope, then crossing it by crossing my hands, and just being a very flashy boxer with it. Afterwards a lot of inmates gave me more respect.

Late one afternoon, I was on a punchbag and this big bloke started to hit the bag next to me. He then asked me to show him how to punch correctly, which I did for a bit. I asked him (as every inmate always does, when meeting you for the first time) what he was in for. He told me he was a lifer and in for murder. He stayed in the big house with the other lifers, who were all getting prepared to be released in the coming months back into society. There was something about him that I didn't like. It was just my instincts telling me he was a wrong-un. He asked me if he could meet me in the gym later that evening for some boxing lessons. I said no, I could not do that as I was not a trained coach, and I just liked to keep myself to myself whilst doing my training. He accepted my excuse, but I could tell from the way he looked at me, that he knew I just didn't want to be around him.

I met lifers before on several occasions, and their past crimes never bothered me as I did not think about them. However, I just got a very uneasy feeling in the presence of this bloke, and I thought, *what about the family of the person he killed?* I imagined the parents, brothers, sisters, and children. What if they were in my position and this close to the person they despised, who they would gladly set on fire? I only saw him again on a couple of occasions, and we just nodded to each other. I was happy with that.

I also met another inmate I kept my distance from, not because I thought he was dangerous, but because he had confided in me that he was an ex-prison officer. We were sitting next to each other in a small classroom having a discussion with a prison psychologist. The debate was whether violent people had been cruel to animals when they were young. They had much evidence to say yes, they did show signs of cruelty from an early age. I loved animals, however I can admit to torturing earthworms by putting them onto the very hot bonnet of a car in the summer and watching them wriggle about and go all crusty and hard under the hot sun rays. I wouldn't call that being cruel to animals, though. This bloke said something during the debate that made me think he had been in the police force, and I turned and looked at him for a bit. He noticed this, and afterwards he confided in me about his work as a prison officer. I told him it made no difference to me. I would not be his best pal; however, I would also not say anything to anyone. I figured the other inmates would find out soon enough by themselves.

With the prison being in Lincolnshire, which is the flattest county in England as it has no hills or mountains, the RAF tested aeroplanes nearby. Quite often fighter jets would scream across the sky, flying low over the prison. Some of the inmates were from up north, and many came from HMP Leeds in the Armley area, and many others came from Salford, near Manchester. There were only a couple of us cockneys, but no one bothered us.

I met inmates who had been in other prisons, and they had met people that I knew. One of them had just come from HMP Gartree, Leicestershire. He told me about meeting the notorious cop killer from Shepherd's Bush, London. I did not know him.

He said, "He told me to ask him one question, then to leave him alone. Apparently, it's what he tells everyone when they first meet him." This inmate asked him how it felt to have spent so long banged up inside.

He replied, "If I had done it a year earlier, they would have hanged me, so at least I've had a life inside."

I then told him about an old bricklayer I worked with who had been on a job at the end of the road and heard the shots. There were a few tough lads in the prison, and others who thought they were tough, but they could only be in a gang. I thought of them as arseholes with no bottle. Anything I had ever done, I had done on my own. I didn't need the safety of a gang. One young lad I got on well with had a small semi-circular scar running up through his eyebrow and to the top of his forehead. He told me it happened when he had a falling-out with another drug dealer, and as they wrestled, this bloke got him in a headlock and tried to shoot him in the head with the hand gun he was holding, but he jerked his head back and the bullet just grazed along his forehead. Another inmate was addicted to ironing. He would be asking all the cons if they had any clothes that needed ironing. He told me he was doing ten years for firearm offences, and he now only had a year to go. He found ironing to be a form of escapism and relaxation.

One thing I liked about North Sea Camp was having my own key. I could come and go during the day and go out for walks around the prison land that went right along to near the coast, with the sea not far in the distance. I could sit talking to the sheep on the other side of a low wire fence, with their baby lambs running about playing. I could see big trawler-type boats sitting out at sea. Being out in the fresh air was exhilarating for me, but make no mistake I was still in prison, and nothing could be harder than keeping yourself within the prison boundary. I had mates who had done loads of prison time, and they all said there was no way they could go to an open prison, as they would be off at the first chance they got. They wouldn't have the discipline to do the time surrounded by open fields.

Having your liberty taken from you is the most mind-numbing thing anyone can experience. On visiting day each week, all the inmates would sit on top of a grass hill near the prison canteen. You could see the visitors being led in from prison minibuses that collected visitors from the train station. My parents had made the arduous journey all the way from West London to Boston, Lincolnshire, and on a Sunday. I felt very guilty, as any bad son should, making them struggle through a journey that took them nearly all day, and they would not get home until late that night, and all because of me being an idiot.

We had a great one-hour visit, and it was so nice to see friendly familiar faces in this hostile environment. Other inmates who did not have visits were doing the waiting on the tables, with tea or coffee and biscuits. The lad who loved ironing was waiting on us, and I told my parents about his story. My father said, "Best of luck to him," and smiled. I think my mum was relieved by seeing me so cheerful, and I made sure I told her how well I was doing. My dad understood perfectly when I explained about having my skipping rope sent in, and how it had gained me some respect.

One week later I heard from Gabby that a few friends were visiting me from my local pub. The following Sunday, I was sitting on the bank waiting for the visitors. The other inmates were waving to their visitors as they caught sight of them coming in and running off down the hill to get into the canteen. As the group of us on the hill got smaller and smaller, I thought, *they are not coming. They probably got very drunk the night before and overslept.* There were only two of us left on the hill, and the other lad was waiting for his wife and kids to come, poor sod, as they never did turn up. My mates finally came through the gates, accompanied by a screw. I shouted out, "Don't let them in, they are carrying weapons and drugs."

That scared them, even though they weren't carrying anything apart from their very heavy heads from the late night of drinking. They apologised for being so late, and we only got fifteen minutes for a chat, then they had the long journey all the way back to London, silly sods.

Finally, my last day arrived. Whilst inside you see lots of inmates having their last day, and it gives you hope, as you know one day it will be you in that position. You wish them good luck and tell them not to come back. It's a tradition that you must eat your breakfast on the last day, or they say you'll come back for it. I ate every bit of mine, then I had to do the rounds, with my form of departure getting a signature from each prison officer in charge of each section of the prison. They would not let you leave until you had the form fully signed up. I said my goodbyes, collected my belongings that I had arrived in on my first day, and I was escorted out of the prison and into a waiting area, as I was being picked up by one of my bosses.

Whilst waiting on my own, this screw came in and started to question me about various other inmates. I knew what he was doing, and I was never a grass, and I would not give him any information he was looking for. He was looking for a promotion, slippery fucker. It was great to drive away from there, and I thanked my boss, as they had been terrific to me and Gabby through the whole bad experience.

The one thing I learnt about a bad experience is that it usually happens to you for a reason. I wouldn't suggest going to prison just to experience the feeling of being released from prison, but it was the most incredible feeling ever. If I hadn't been put away, I would never have been given the opportunity to experience that feeling. I had learnt my lesson. I was smart enough to know that I would never be coming back there. I fought the law and the law won! My boss drove me to the company head office so I could collect my car. What a strange experience to be in a car driving on the M25 on a Friday afternoon, having just been released from prison that morning, and having not seen a car for six weeks, let alone actually driven one and amongst this mad traffic on a Friday afternoon. It is amazing that drivers are just so unaware of other drivers' personal circumstances. Drivers were overtaking me and looking at me, but they had no idea that I had woken up that morning in prison.

When I got home, Gabby and Daniel were waiting for me, and it was a special reunion. Later that evening, Gabby looked at me sitting there looking at the clock and said, "Why don't you go down to the pub and see your mates for a few drinks?"

Just as she finished the sentence, I was out the door, in the car and off. When I arrived at the pub, everyone was elated to see me, but they still took the piss that I had been given such a short sentence. I explained that I was proud to have stayed out of prison for so long, and to only get a short sentence, that was called being smart in my book. We had a great and very long night, with me not getting home until Saturday midday. I went straight to bed to sleep and then went back out again Saturday night.

I don't know how Gabby put up with me then – I was a bit of a tit. Most people reading this would assume that getting home from a prison sentence, I would want immediate sexual pleasure, but it's hard to explain when your mind is elsewhere. I was surrounded by people using cocaine, and that becomes your replacement for sex. Don't listen to these people who bang on about having fantastic sex whilst high on cocaine – it just doesn't happen, believe me. I found cocaine blocks a lot of blood movement around the body, and to get an erection, men need extra blood going to the penis to enlarge it. I found it very difficult to get an erection when on a cocaine binge. This causes the group of men who are taking it together and enjoying the male company to be without any sexual distractions. You all go back to a hotel room and drink more and more. Some may discuss sex and even put a sex channel on the TV, but most of the conversations are about the life of crime, villains we all knew, and their funny experiences. We may even do a bit of shadow-boxing for a laugh. Then, when you eventually get home, you sleep and sleep. I was lucky, as I mentioned before. I had associated cocaine use with staying less drunk and more in control, and not falling about the place. This also allowed me to section it off to weekends only. Come Monday morning, I was back at work and completely focused on my work. Never once did I ever let it interfere with my decision making or my work. They were different worlds, and I made sure I kept them miles apart.

Chapter Eleven
Making Amends and Seeing the World

A couple of weeks later I was back at work. I was now a contracts manager, visiting sites for my bosses. I had made my mind up that I was done with getting into trouble with the law. From now on, I was a lover, not a fighter. I would put all my energies into giving Gabby, Daniel, and James a better life. In 1998 I was looking after an extension to the Windsor Leisure Centre, which was a very interesting project, with green face blocks and acoustic blockwork. I met a visiting contracts manager from the main contractor, and he explained to me how he was working on a fascinating project to build a large wheel to be placed in central London opposite Parliament on the river Thames. He explained how it would never stop and would rotate continuously, very slowly, for people to get on and get off. At the top, you'd be able to see all over London. He was nervous for this coming weekend, as they would be lifting the wheel to secure it into its permanent place. I saw him the following week, and he was very happy that everything had gone well, but it would be a few months before the public would be allowed on it.

My bosses asked me if I would like to open a western office, near the town of Bristol, for them. I would have complete control over the office and finding work using the company's good reputation.

I said, "Yes, I would love to have a go at that." I found an office to rent, and I found a house to rent not far away. I fitted the office out, and I started to price tenders for sites in the area. My bosses were on the end of the phone with constant good advice for things I wasn't quite sure of, usually specific rates for items of work in the bill of quantities (BQ). I won my first couple of projects, and everything was going well, with them just sending down the wages each week that I could then distribute to the men.

It was now 1999, and we had sold our house in London to allow Gabby and Daniel to move in with me. We soon found a nice detached three-bedroom house to buy. We moved in March 2000 into our new home. It was at the bottom of a quiet cul-de-sac with a detached garage and all very private. We had great neighbours, and it was all very different to living in London. We were happy, and I was working hard building some good contracts for my bosses in London. I decided to get another Staffordshire bull terrier. I called a number from an advert in *Dog World* newspaper, which covered all the dog shows and had good breeders selling correctly registered puppies. I arranged to go to a place called Dudley in the Midlands to choose a puppy from a litter. When I got there, the owners were very nice, and they showed me both the mother and the father, then these four little eight-week-old puppies came in and were running about. One of them kept going under me from behind, as I was crouching down near to the floor, and then he would jump up and lick my hand. I said, "He'll do."

It is true what they say: "A puppy picks you; you do not pick the puppy." I got him home, and Gabby and Daniel were very excited with the new arrival to our family. We called him Jock, after the film *Jock of the Bushveld*, which was about a runt puppy who is saved from being drowned by a rancher and then brought up in South Africa. A great film for Staffordshire bull terrier lovers.

My boss called me one day in the summer, and he told me he had been invited to a garden party at Lambeth Palace, London, but he couldn't make it and would I like to go in his place with my wife to represent the company. I said, "I'd be delighted to go, and I'm sure Gabby would be happy to accompany me."

We had never been to a garden party before. I thought it would be great just to see what goes on in those posh circles. Lambeth Palace is a glorious old building and the home to the Archbishop of Canterbury, with the second-largest garden in London, second only to Buckingham Palace. We arrived in suitable posh attire, and we were greeted by the Archbishop of Canterbury himself with a warm hello and welcome. All they do at garden parties is mingle on the manicured lawns with flutes of champagne in hand, all the while being waited on by servants walking about holding silver trays up high, with small tiny sandwiches on and fresh salmon. We spoke to a few people who were high up in the construction industry, and some from the London Corporation and the greater London council, who were big clients of the construction industry, and the main contractor who had arranged this get-together.

I liked watching the brass quartet playing nice, mellow background music. My biggest disappointment was feeling so out of place, and in such a tranquil setting on a Friday afternoon in central London. Don't they realise there is rush-hour traffic on the other side of that garden wall, and homeless people selling *The Big Issue.* It just all seemed so unreal to me. We made our excuses and left after a couple of hours, and I had done some good PR work for my boss. When we walked across the lawns and finally got to the main palace building, Gabby took out her flat shoes from her bag and said, "My feet are killing me in these heels." She lit up a cigarette – no smoking at the garden party – as she was putting on her shoes, and as she did the archbishop walked around the corner and nearly fell over her. Gabby looked up with fag in mouth and said, "Sorry, mate, just getting me flats on." I was speechless, but the archbishop smiled warmly and just walked on, like it happened every day to him. What a nice man.

We got to the end of 2001, and one main contractor went bust on us. My bosses told me, "Roger, come back to London, as we are closing down the western office now." I had to think about it long and hard. I decided I would have a go at being the subcontractor myself. I had learnt loads, and I just knew I would be good at it. Look at the life I had lived up to now. Why couldn't I look after a load of bricklayers on a few sites? I had been pricing all the works and winning the contracts on my own. My bosses were great and wished me well.

I still had my limited company from 1985, and I had changed its name in 1998 for a situation just like this one I was now in. I spoke with another main contractor, which had taken over the site where the other company had gone bust, as they were now going to be finishing the project over the next year. They appointed my new company to do the brickwork package on a daywork basis, which meant I couldn't lose any money. I spoke to the men who had been working with me under the London bosses, and I explained what was happening and offered them the work. They accepted the jobs, and I was up and running now. I had a couple of other small projects of my own on the go as well, and it was tough for the first year or so, as many times me and Gabby had no wages at all coming in.

I had been using the London bosses' quantity surveyor (QS), who drove down to carry out the valuations for me. He was a freelance QS, so it worked well. We struggled through a short period, and two years later we rented an office in central Cardiff. The company was doing well, and I felt the freelance QS should now be working with me full time on PAYE as a director, and not as a freelancer anymore, so I gave him forty-eight shares in the company, free of charge. He was very happy, and we started a very good working relationship. We are still very good friends today.

The company was building more and more of the southwest and Wales, and they were all getting new buildings with the brick, stone, and blockwork built by our company. We were also making money, which was nice. Gabby and Daniel were doing well, and they loved living in our new house and new location. My son James would still come over a couple of times a year to stay with us, which was great. He had done well at school and at colleges, before moving over to England to get a degree in quantity surveying. His graduation day was very special, and I was very proud of him. His mother and her brother and family came over for it. We had a good day and a nice meal in a restaurant afterwards.

Daniel was also doing well at school, and he was a very good footballer and drummer now. He got picked out whilst playing in a Sunday league match by a scout from a professional team. I took him to train at their school of excellence for six weeks. He played for them in matches against Cardiff and then against Portsmouth. The head coach explained to us that Daniel was very good and had a fantastic attitude, but he wasn't any better than what he already had, so he couldn't offer Daniel a contract. Daniel was fine about it, and I told him he had given it his best, and in football quite often it's all about 'if your face fits'. I think that's when Daniel decided to concentrate more on his drumming, and he was excellent at it. I had joined the Buffs – the Royal Antediluvian Order of Buffaloes – as I had been told it was a good organisation that would raise lots of money for local charities and good causes. As their motto went, 'You only have one right as a Buff, and that is the right to give'. The club building had a nice social club at the front for local people, and a hall at the back for the Buffs meetings. Everyone at the club and the Buffs were nice people, and I enjoyed my time there. Unfortunately, as time moved on, most of the members who were quite elderly died, and it saddened me to be going to frequent funerals. I stopped going.

Meanwhile, back at work, I was enjoying my new position of being the subcontractor with no one above me. The buck stopped with me. We were doing well, and in 2006 we bought a freehold office building. We had two ladies working full time, one on the ground floor as the receptionist and head of admin, with the second lady on the first floor as head of payroll and accounts. I was based on the second floor in the largest office, with the kitchen and toilet up on the third floor. After a few years, my QS and fellow director divorced his wife in London. He moved into my office to share it with me, and it worked well. He met a nice lady and moved in with her. They were very happy, and they eventually got married.

Gabby was still having lots of problems with her stomach and the Crohn's disease, which meant she would not go away on holiday. I had to go away on my own; she didn't mind this, and she looked forward to the DVDs I'd bring back, to show her the places I visited. I visited Toronto, Canada, and whilst there I jumped on a plane to New York. It was only for two days, but I got to see all the sights, and I had a very special memory. When I checked in to the Marriott Hotel on Broadway, the lady receptionist said, "When you get into your room, open the curtains and call me."

I went up in the elevator to floor 42. I entered the room and put down my bag. I walked over to the large window and opened the curtains. I was looking straight down Broadway to Times Square, with all the lights on, as it was late now. I called the receptionist.

She said, "What do you think of the view?"

I thanked her and said it was amazing. On my last day, I had checked out of my hotel, and I travelled south on the subway to get the ferry boat over to Ellis Island. This is where historically all the new arrivals coming to New York to seek employment and a future had to be processed and either allowed in or turned away. Then I jumped back on to the ferry to go on to Liberty Island to see the statue of Liberty. They weren't letting anyone inside the statue as a parachutist had got caught up on the crown of the statue that morning. I bought an ice cream and laid down on the grass, using my bag as a pillow. The view back to New York was terrific, with all the different boats travelling across the water, and the large bridge from Brooklyn to Lower Manhattan. The iconic Twin Towers in all their glory stood proud, high above the Financial District.

This was at the end of August 2001, and ten days later, two airplanes flew into the Twin Towers in a terrorist attack. I often wondered if anyone was doing the same as I had on that morning of 9/11 and if, from that same spot on the grass I'd enjoyed, they'd watched with horror as the two planes flew into the towers. I am very relieved it didn't happen on the day I was there, and I would not have liked to see it happen. I have a photo of me standing between two New York policemen in Times Square. A third policeman took the photo. I thought after the attack that may have been their last photo, and I wondered if I should send it to the NYPD, because if they had been killed in the 9//11 attack, their families would appreciate it, but I never sent it. We had the picture on the wall of a London pub for a while, as all the villains thought it was hilarious to see me between two coppers and smiling.

A couple of years later, I had a great week in Las Vegas. I went mainly to see Oscar De La Hoya box against the German boxer Felix Sturm for the middleweight WBO title at the MGM Grand Hotel. Also on the bill was Bernard Hopkins, who was another world middleweight champion. If they both won, they would set up a bout between the two of them later that year. Oscar De La Hoya would also be setting a world record for the most world titles at different weights, having already been world champion at super featherweight, lightweight, light-welterweight, welterweight, and light-middleweight. He was now trying to add middleweight to his list of world titles, a phenomenal achievement that he achieved with a win on points.

Whilst at the fight, I got to shake Mike Tyson's hand. I approached him and put out my hand. He shook, it and I said, "I'm Roger the boxer from London. From everyone in London, we wish you well."

Don't ask me why I said that – it just blurted out, as I was a bit star-struck.

He lent towards me and he almost whispered, "Thank you very much."

Then I noticed the old movie star Tony Curtis, in a white suit with a cowboy hat on and a young dolly bird model hanging from each arm. Very Hollywood. I put out my hand, and I said, "Nice to meet you, Mr Curtis. I'm Roger the boxer from London. My mum loved all your films."

What a crap thing to say. He smiled and said, whilst exaggerating a great cockney accent, "Roger the boxer from London, it's nice to meet you too."

What a gentleman. They also announced there was a pop star there standing near Tony Curtis called Beyoncé. I had never heard of her. Don't forget it was 2004, though, and I was forty-four years old, so I just walked past her.

Las Vegas was an amazing place. I went to see some fantastic shows like the Blue Man Group and the magician David Copperfield. I went on a bus trip to the Hoover Dam and then took a boat ride around the lake that's held back by the dam called Lake Mead. I think it is the largest manmade lake in the world. We visited a small workers' village where the men stayed whilst constructing the dam and blowing the tunnels through the rocks on either side, to divert the Colorado River whilst the dam was in construction. It was sad to learn so many men had lost their lives whilst building the dam.

I then bought a ticket for a helicopter tour over the Grand Canyon. They collected me from the MGM Hotel in a stretch limo. What else? This was Las Vegas! I got into the helicopter beside the pilot in the front. There was a couple in the back.

The pilot said, "It's your lucky day as I have to drop off some supplies down beside the river to the locals today." What surprised me, having never been in a helicopter before, was that he went up to only about two metres from the ground, and then he moved straight along the runway following the white line in the centre, and he lifted and curved the helicopter up to the right and into the sky.

We were all wearing headphones, and the spaghetti Western music was playing in our ears, which was fantastic. I was filming with my DVD camera thinking, *this will be great with the music playing as well.* I had forgotten the music was only to us via the headphones and my DVD recording just had the noise of the helicopter engines as background noise. Doh!

As he promised, we went over this mountain ridge, and there in front of us was the most amazing sight of the entire Grand Canyon in front of us. What amazed me about the helicopter was that we seemed to be travelling so slow, at times I thought we were just going to drop from the sky. He took the helicopter down and landed alongside the fast-moving rapids of the Colorado River – what a sight. The pilot stayed sitting, and we heard people taking things out of the rear side door of the helicopter. Then they waved to us, and he took the helicopter back up to about two metres above the water of the river, and then he accelerated along the river. Now I could see just how fast it travelled, and I realised it was because I now had something stationary to compare it to, and boy was it fast. Then we swooped upwards into the sky and back to the Las Vegas landing runway.

Over these years I got to see a lot more places every bit as good as Las Vegas, like Barbados, where I chartered a fishing boat and crew. I always had this passion to see blue marlin fish. I didn't really want to catch one, as they are huge and very dangerous. I just loved the sight of them jumping out of the water, with their sail fins and long pointed nose like a swordfish. What I didn't realise was how clever they were – they were a very difficult fish to see or catch. I got to swim with turtles and saw some small flying fish come out of the water, spread their wings, and then fly above the water for about twenty yards before diving back in. I eventually caught a fish, and it was a whopper of a wahoo fish, which is also known as a king fish.

I stayed in a very nice five-star hotel, but I wanted to see the famous posh hotel where a lot of the big showbiz stars stayed. I got a taxi to the front security gate of this hotel, and I told the security man, "I'd like a tour of the hotel, as I was thinking of returning next month with my wife." He made a call, and a manager came out and told me to return later that evening, at about 7:00 p.m., and he would walk me around the hotel.

I returned all nicely turned out, and this manager gave me an in-depth tour of the marvellous hotel, and we even went into the suites where the stars usually stayed, and he explained to me how one of the famous stars even brings his own chef everywhere he goes. At the end, I thanked him, and I asked if I could stay and eat in their restaurant.

He said, "But of course, make yourself comfortable in the bar, and we will call you whcn a table is ready for you."

I was sitting at the empty bar when this couple came in and introduced themselves to me. They were laughing and had already had a bit to drink. I asked them where they came from, and the bloke said, "I'm a cockney from Canary Wharf."

I smiled and said, "You can't tell me you went to school and you were brought up in Canary Wharf."

He replied, "Oh no, I was brought up in Hampshire and I'm a banker."

"Really," I said. "So, you are a complete merchant banker, then."

They both replied in unison, "Oh yes, we are complete merchant bankers."

That made me laugh, as they were not aware that *merchant banker* was rhyming slang for *wanker* where I came from. It was nice to get a little dig in for the working classes.

The meal was fabulous, and I could see why the stars stayed there. The only disappointment I had with Barbados was when I walked from my hotel into Bridgetown. It was just like the area I went to school in. There were wooden boxes all along the side of the road like an untidy marketplace. The boxes were full of green bananas, yams, and other fruits. It was still a lovely place, and you couldn't fault the sandy beaches.

It was very much like Mauritius in the Indian Ocean. I loved it, and I had a very relaxing week there. Once again, I chartered my own boat and crew. We went right out into the Indian Ocean heading towards Madagascar. When I looked back, you could barely see Mauritius. We saw a large whale with her calf swimming, and I caught six fish. All of them were skipjacks – tuna. They were all about 10kg. When we got back, I told the skipper he could have them to sell to the local hotels.

I also had a great holiday going to see my sister Molly and my brother-in-law Kevin in New Zealand. It was a long journey that I decided to break up. I stayed at the Bel-Air Hotel in Hollywood, in California, for three days on my way over, and on the way back I stopped in San Francisco for three days. I had a tour of the stars' houses in Hollywood, which was good fun, especially seeing where Elvis stayed whilst making all his films. When you walk along Sunset Boulevard in the sun, looking at all the palm trees lining the road, it makes you understand why wealthy stars flock to live there.

San Francisco was good on my way back from New Zealand, especially the tour of Alcatraz Prison. They have cells in complete darkness they call 'the hole'. You step inside a cell that is inside another cell and close both doors, and all you have whilst in complete darkness is the voice in your headphones.

It's an old inmate telling you, "You are now in the hole. I spent three months in here in 1952. I would pull off one of the buttons from my top and toss it in the air, then spend time trying to find it. I got so good at finding it, I had to spin myself around and around several times to make it more difficult, but even then, I could go straight to it after a few days. I would pretend there was a TV in the corner of the room, and I would walk over to sit in the opposite corner, then get up and walk back across the room to turn it over to another channel, to watch something else."

It was great to hear the actual voice of someone who had experienced that. It made me think, as I walked out of the hole, just how easy I had had it when I was in prison – there was no comparison. Of all the American cities I've been to, I felt San Francisco was the most American. That may sound a bit silly, but it just made me feel it was so American compared to everywhere else, with the roads on steep hills, buildings with outside metal stairways on the front and alongside the main roads, the trams and their tracks everywhere, the flat crossroad junctions I'd seen watching car chases on TV, water hydrants shooting water high into the air on pavements, Macy's department store, and the Golden Gate Bridge.

I had a great time in New Zealand with my sister and her family. They have all done very well out there and are now very settled and having a great way of life for all the children as well. Whilst there, I visited Christchurch on the South Island. It's great going on the boat from Wellington to Picton on the South Island through what is called ‘the sounds’. It is absolutely quiet and probably the most peaceful place on earth – just the humming of the boat engine and the calm water amongst the high hills either side of you. Very tranquil.

One of my best holidays was to South Africa. I flew to Cape Town and stayed in the six-star One&Only Hotel right in the marina, with a great view from my balcony to Table Mountain. It was a very interesting place with very friendly people. I went out to Robben Island and the prison where Nelson Mandela was kept. His cell was very small with a thin mattress on the floor. I caught the cable car up to the top of Table Mountain. Whilst there I phoned my parents.

My father was very happy and said, “I’ve taken calls from lots of places but never Table Mountain, Cape Town.”

I got the hotel to provide an S-Class Mercedes and driver to take me up the coast to see some whales. The driver was great and waited as I went out on a whale-watching boat. We saw three large whales, and they all went deep, putting their tails high in the air. It was a great thing to see live. Then, on the way back to shore, we were surrounded by about thirty dolphins swimming at great speed all around the boat and going under it as well. *Fantastic!*

The following morning, I caught the Blue Train to Johannesburg and Pretoria, where I was going to stay for two days. I had heard lots about this luxury train, and I wasn’t disappointed with the opulence. I had a large cabin with a sofa that pulled out to form a bed, a leather Chesterfield armchair with a wooden table, a lamp, and a TV high up on the wall with an en suite bathroom that had a full-length bath with 21-carat gold taps and the floor in Italian marble. When the train got going, I went out to explore. I passed through the long bar and restaurant and got to the very last carriage, which was like an old gentleman’s club in Mayfair London, complete with leather chairs and sofas and deep carpet. The whole end wall of the train was a window, looking out to the rails behind us.

I sat down and enjoyed chatting to some of the other passengers. They were all very nice, and a few of them were what you would call upper class, with others that seemed just like me, but probably with a much nicer history than me. I returned to my cabin, and I thought I’d have a bath. What an experience that was. I filled the bath right up with all smelly bubble bath in it. As I lay in the bath, I opened the Venetian blinds to the large window. I was now looking out at open fields with some hills in the distance. A large group of wild ostriches was running in the field. I took a moment to savour this. Here I was soaking in a luxury bath full of bubbles with 21-carat gold taps, an Italian marble floor, and a fantastic view of wild ostriches, and *I was on a train!* I just couldn't believe it, and I doubt if I will ever experience a feeling like it ever again, soaking in the hot water completely relaxed, and on a train.

As we approached Johannesburg, we passed a very large township made up of thousands of corrugated iron shelters, and many oil drums spouting fire, with a dozen men sitting around them and waving to us. *Why aren't they at work, out shopping, or indoors watching TV?* I wondered. But this is their life, sitting by a bonfire in an old oil drum surrounded by a couple of square miles of old shacks thrown together out of corrugated iron. I couldn't see how, if they came home drunk from the pub, they would find their shack amongst the thousands of other shacks, which all looked the same and were all joined up together. It was amazing, and it reminded me of how lucky I was.

I had a good night's sleep, and the train pulled into Pretoria at midday the following day. I had been warned about the high crime rate in Joburg, and I knew I would have to keep vigilant being on my own. When I checked into my hotel and the receptionist said to keep safe and try not to look like a tourist, I thought that may be difficult walking around with a DVD camera, but I got away with it, and I didn't get bothered by anyone. I saw a few groups of dodgy characters near the ATM machines and traffic lights, but they ignored me. I thought maybe they knew I was Roger the Boxer, and I laughed out loud.

The next day I had a car and driver booked to take me to Sun City, which was very good to see with its own zoo, beach, swimming pools, and casino. It was where they held large sporting events like international boxing.

On the journey, the driver said, "If we get stopped and they have guns, just give them what they want and they will let us drive away. If you argue, they will shoot you."

I thought, *Charming.* Good fortune smiled on us, as we didn't get stopped either direction thankfully. Along the route I saw platinum mines and silver mines, also large private estates owned by the wealthy South Africans who many years ago would have had many slaves working on these estates for them. The following morning a car took me to the airport to get a small plane to Kruger National Park. It was only forty-five minutes in the air with the propellers turning away. I arrived at the Kruger, and I was escorted to a nice detached villa with a thatched pointed roof. It had a separate large bedroom, a living room, and a large en suite bathroom with a bath and a shower. French doors opened to reveal two large sofas on the patio, with small tables beside them and an outdoor shower.

There was grass in front of the patio going all the way down for about a hundred yards to a river that ran across in front of trees – a fantastic view.

I was only there for three days, but that was plenty of time for me to see all the big cats, elephants, rhinos, hippos, zebras, impalas, wildebeests, giraffes, crocodiles, and lots of baboons. You go out on safari very early in the mornings, about 5:00 a.m. It's very exciting, and on our second day we got very close to a leopard who crawled up to our jeep using the back wheel below me as cover. He was going to attack the impalas behind us. As he crouched just a foot below me, I was filming him, and he looked up with those big yellow eyes, and I thought he was going to jump up at me, but he must have thought I was too fat. Then a wildebeest let out a roar in the distance, and the impalas scattered, and the leopard just walked away from us.

When we got back to the main building for lunch, we were all very excited about the leopard, and the main gamekeeper told me, "I have never seen anyone get that close to a wild leopard before. They just don't usually come that close to our jeeps."

I felt very lucky, but the show wasn't over. I was escorted back to my villa, and when I entered, there was this massive baboon sitting on the sideboard in my living room with the glass jar full of nuts in his hand next to the fruit bowl. When the shock had subsided, I walked very slowly across to the French double doors and slowly opened them up wide.

I then walked back to behind the baboon, and I told him, "You shouldn't be in here," and I moved quickly towards him. Luckily, he jumped down and ran out the double doors carrying an apple and the glass jar full of nuts. I grabbed my DVD camera, and I managed to film him on the patio before he ran and jumped up and over the garden wall.

I showed the DVD to the gamekeeper, who laughed and said, "That's why we tell you to keep your windows and doors securely shut when you are out on safari."

On the safari on the next day, the ranger guide said, "Who wants to get out of the jeep and walk with me for the rest of the way back to base?"

A man with his two grown-up sons and me were the only volunteers. It was great to be walking through the bushes, not knowing what you may come across. We came to a clearing with a herd of wildebeests maybe fifty yards ahead of us, and about six elephants. The ranger showed us this small white cloth bag he had. He held it up, and it was only about three inches wide and tied at the top. He told us how this would save our lives should we come too close to the elephants, as they killed more people than any other wild animal. He shook the small bag, which was full of powder, and the powder came out in a small cloud and travelled away in the breeze, telling the ranger the direction of the wind. Luckily, it was going away from the animals ahead of us. That meant we were downwind from them, and they could not smell us. I returned home after an exhilarating ten-day holiday in South Africa, with some great memories to keep forever.

The next holiday I went on was to Beijing, Hong Kong, and Singapore. Beijing was interesting with its history, Tiananmen Square, the Summer Palace, Forbidden City, and of course the iconic Great Wall of China. I visited the Great Wall, a car and driver collecting me from my hotel to take me there. When the car pulled up, there was another man in the back. He said he was my guide and would see that I was properly looked after, because the driver spoke no English. After a while I asked this guide, "Is it true you eat dogs?"

He replied, "We are poor people. We have to eat, and the dogs are bred just for eating, just like you have cows or sheep. Would you like to go to a market to see the dogs being bought?"

I respectfully declined. We arrived at a place called Badaling, the tourist entrance to the Great Wall. It really does take your breath away, and you just cannot believe it is manmade. I walked along the Great Wall of China amongst the hundreds of Chinese tourists. They do not need Western visitors; they can get by with their own tourists. Hundreds of years ago when they were building the wall, at times it could be thirty degrees below freezing, and many of them died. If a worker ran away from it, they would kill the whole of his family – every generation.

The following day I was in Tiananmen Square; it was by far the largest square I have ever been to, and it was full of Chinese tourists. I did not see many Westerners like me. There was this long queue, and I mean very long, stretching from this small building all the way down one side of the square and out of sight, and it was four people wide with a space of about ten feet, then a rope – like a moat around a castle – and soldiers positioned every ten metres along it. This was to create a large gap between the soldiers and the queue, like a no man's land, to stop anyone from joining the queue other than at the end of it.

It was a queue to see Chairman Mao's body. They have his body on display in a glass coffin. Every day they raise it up from below, where it is kept in ice overnight. The way the coffin is positioned, they say he rises in the East and sets in the West, like the sun. I walked along it a bit, holding my DVD camera and filming it, avoiding all the sellers of individual red roses, when this little bloke came up to me and said in a quiet voice, in broken English, "You want to get in to see without queue?"

I said, "Okay."

"First you must store your camera."

We went across the road to another small building where you could leave your camera and anything else not allowed whilst visiting the tomb. I gave him the money he wanted (about £20), and he walked with me back to the front of the queue. We got to about three metres from the front. The nearest soldier was about ten metres away from us, and this bloke said, "Quick," and he pushed me under the rope and into the queue. The soldier turned towards us, but this little man just said something in Chinese and waved to him, and the soldier turned away.

Now I was making the queue five deep, and the Chinese people in the queue were not happy. It was handy they were all much smaller than me. I just ignored them and pretended to be stupid and not understand. When we reached the entrance, the queue had to divide, with two people going to the right of the glass coffin, and two going to the left of it. I just pushed the little bloke beside me out of the way, and a steward made him drop in behind me to see the coffin. They kept you moving slowly past the coffin, and the Chinese visitors were throwing their red roses at the coffin, and the roses were landing on the floor.

There must have been a two-foot mound of red roses. We were out the other side in about three minutes. I thought the whole experience was most bizarre. Why queue for so long for just three minutes to see a dead body? Pay money for red roses, then throw them at a coffin? I'm sure they collect the roses up at the end of the evening and sell them all again the next day. I laughed when I thought of the little man who put me in the queue, the Chinese Del Boy.

I flew from Beijing to Hong Kong, as I wanted to see the Hong Kong Sevens rugby tournament. Hong Kong is very different to Beijing. In Beijing you saw no Western cars, only Japanese or Korean cars, whereas Hong Kong was full of BMWs and Mercs. I had a great time at the seven-a-side rugby game, and my hotel very generously allowed me to sit in their private box at the stadium. I noticed this very attractive and very elegant Asian lady looking at me. She approached me and put out her hand and introduced herself. I cannot remember her name. We chatted with the usual small talk and about Hong Kong and the rugby.

She then said, "Nice to have met you, Roger," and she went back to the hotel executive she had been speaking with. A man from the hotel approached me and said, "That lady you were just talking with is the best head-hunter in this region." Apparently, they fly her in when one large company wants to head-hunt a top executive or chairman from a rival company to join them. They bring her in to make it happen discreetly, from the first approach to the conclusion, and she gets paid a vast sum of money. I never knew there was a profession called head-hunting – you learn something new every day. Another guest in the private box approached me. He was from Thailand, but he spoke with a soft American accent. We got talking about Thailand, and I explained that I had never been there, mainly because in our pub many years ago in West London we had a group of about six men who worked on the post for Royal Mail. They would go to Thailand twice a year and would openly admit to having fun with the lady boys there. We used to call them the 'pervy posties'. This man found all of this very amusing, and then explained to me how the best parts of Thailand were right down to the bottom of the coastline, where he owned two large hotels.

He then said quietly to me, "Why don't you plan a visit and stay at my hotel? I will give you a suite free of charge, and you will be my special guest."

I don't know why, but my 'young kid off the streets of London' streetwise instincts suddenly kicked in, and I respectfully declined his kind offer. He just smiled and walked away. I am sure he was probably very genuine and would have been a fine holiday host, but I just felt it was a bit too much man-to-man closeness for me. It may have been his beige-coloured suit, yellow cravat, and yellow socks with white shoes that worried me.

On my last night before flying to Singapore to see two of my friends, I was feeling very lonely and I was having a drink at a bar. This local girl came up and sat beside me. She asked me to buy her a drink, which I did. I was attracted to her because of the size of her breasts. They were bigger than I'd ever seen on an Asian lady before.

We had a laugh, chatting for a bit, when two of her friends came up beside us. One of them said, "You two go dance," and pushed us out on to a small dance floor, leaving our drinks on the bar. I had been drinking directly from bottles of Budweiser, and I'd had about eight of them. We finished dancing, and we returned and finished our drinks at the bar. They then said, "Let's all go back to your hotel."

I don't know how it happened, but I just sort of got carried along with it all – loud music, beer, dancing, and women being nice to me – and I had my invincible head on now. I thought, *Why not? It'll be a good laugh*. We arrived back to my hotel, and we were in my room. I paid them the money they asked for from my mini safe, then the girls stripped off and took me into the shower. "We must all be very clean first," they said.

That was the last thing I remember, being in the shower. I woke up with the worst headache I have ever had. The pillow was covered in blood, from a cut on the back of my head. I got out of bed, and I felt very groggy. I looked around and it was like a bomb had hit my room. The place was a mess, with all my clothes and things all over the floor, with the mini safe door wide open. I went over to the safe. My passport and money were all still there; nothing had been taken. I realised I only had about an hour until my car was taking me to the airport to fly to Singapore. I was sick in the toilet, and I felt terrible, but I packed all my belongings as well as I could. I had bought some rugby shirts for friends back home, and they lay on the floor, as the girls had tipped them out of their bags and used the bags to completely empty the room's minibar. The minibar had been full of miniature bottles of champagne, and all the various spirits and soft drinks. That was all they took. How could I have been so stupid?

The flight to Singapore was awful, as I felt sick the whole way there, and this young bloke sitting in the seat next to me was eating like he was never going to see food ever again. We hit a massive thunderstorm, and the plane had to circle above Singapore for an hour, and then land on a runway that had to be reversed to allow our flight to land. This was due to the massive storm and strong winds. It meant the plane could only approach and land safely from the opposite direction. All very scary stuff.

It was great to see my two friends. I explained to them what had happened to me with the girls, and they laughed and said, "Rog, you mug." They explained girls in Hong Kong do it all the time. They know they are on CC cameras entering and leaving the hotels. That is why they do not rob you, or they will get arrested and treated harshly. Instead, they just empty the minibar. The hotel is happy, as you will get billed for using your minibar, and they get paid by you. The girls go back to their place and have a party on you.

"So well done for helping the Hong Kong economy, Roger."

My hotel in Singapore was very nice, and it had an infinity pool up on the third floor looking down onto the river and busy roads and bars below. You could swim right up to the edge and just watch all the boats, commuters, and traffic. It was very relaxing. I had a Singapore Sling cocktail in the place where it had originated, Raffles Hotel. The Long Bar, where it is served, is like going back in time. There are bowls of peanuts everywhere, and you are encouraged to eat the nuts and discard the shells on to the floor. This is a long-held tradition, and the floor is covered in the peanut shells, making a crunching sound when anyone walks over them. I was only there for a couple of days, so I didn't get to see much more of Singapore.

Work was going well, and the company was now one of the best around in the construction industry. We had been voted the No. 1 brickwork contractor in the UK in 2006 by *Construction News*. I was at the event night at the Hilton Hotel, Park Lane, London. I had done loads of work entering the competition – photographing our sites, explaining how all the training of apprentices was so important to me. My whole philosophy of long-term thinking and building something to be proud of. It was a very proud moment to receive the trophy, and the next day I stopped on my way home to see my parents. I showed them the trophy. They were very proud of me, and my father reminded me of when I was little. Each week he would bring home *Construction News*, and it always had a glossy colour pull-out from the digger company JCB, with pictures of their big yellow diggers, and I would stare at them for ages. Here I was years later being selected by that publication as the best brickwork company in the UK.

The following year, 2007, we were voted the No. 1 brickwork contractor in the UK at the highly regarded Brick Awards. The Brick Awards were organised by the Brick Development Association (BDA) with input from the Association of Brickwork Contractors (ABC), and these awards had been around for a very long time. To win this award I had to demonstrate to the judges, who were highly acclaimed architects, brick manufacturers, and top construction people, exactly what makes a first-class company.

I had to put forward three of our contracts, and the judges would visit them to inspect the brickwork. They would also go through the company's records of finance and training. It all took me a lot of time and effort, but I knew it was all very important, and it was to get a foothold in the top section of the construction industry.

Winning these awards was always a very proud moment and one to cherish, for me and my fellow directors. This gave us the respect of the whole industry and made our name with the largest and very best main contractors. We were now getting some very big contracts with these big companies. Hospitality was a big thing at this time, and we treated many people from the largest main contractors to the usual events like the Six Nations rugby games, going to matches in Cardiff, Twickenham, and Dublin. The Cheltenham and Royal Ascot horse racing festivals were good fun.

I decided one year to try something different. I booked a small private plane to take eight people from Cardiff to York races, for the Ebor Festival lady's day. As was the normal for these events, people pulled out at the last minute, and we ended up with only a couple of high-profile people to impress, and the rest were mates. On this occasion, my son James came along with a work colleague of his. We met early at Cardiff airport, and we got on this small jet with its two crew members. When we arrived at Leeds Bradford Airport, there were stretch limousines to take us straight to the course and the hospitality section. We had a fantastic day.

In hindsight, after the racing had finished, it would have been far better to be heading into York town centre to carry on partying with the crowds of people, but our limos took us straight back to the airport, and we were on our way back to Cardiff. As the small aircraft came in towards the Cardiff runway in the dark, it was lurching to one side and twisting, as if it wanted to spin full circle. It was very scary.

I said to a good friend of mine sitting beside me, "It's great sometimes to get out of your comfort zone, isn't it?"

He said, "Rog, I am definitely out of my comfort zone. I'm shitting myself."

We eventually landed okay, and it was surreal being back in the Cardiff town centre pubs telling people we had been in York all day at the races. Many didn't believe us. Another different hospitality event I arranged was to see the Rolling Stones in the Cardiff Millennium Stadium in a private box. They were fantastic, and our guests loved it.

In 2010 my father was in hospital. I visited my father, and they told us there was little they could do for him other than to keep him comfortable. He was going to die. I stayed at the hospital beside his bed, along with my sister Freda and my brother Peter. We stayed all night, sleeping in chairs. The hospital had been good and gave my father a private room and allowed us to sleep in the visiting rooms or in the same room as him. After a few days, my other sister arrived all the way from New Zealand, which was great. My brother Steve came in to see him as well.

Some moments my father would wake up and talk to us, then he would just go back to sleep and not wake up again until the following day. It was like this all week. I did get to speak with him on my own, and I told him I was going to get the book he had written published, and his name would be in the British Library forever as an author. This made him smile.

He asked me if everything had been arranged for his funeral back in Ireland, and I said, yes. He smiled and just nodded, saying, "That's fine."

The next day he couldn't speak, but I said to him, "Thank you for being my dad."

He just pointed back to me and then thumped his chest beside his heart, a nice memory I shall always treasure. Having received the last rites twice from a priest, my father passed away, officially from a peptic ulcer leading to pneumonia. It was a large funeral in Ireland with a lot of people there. My cousins had all been fantastic, and it was a great celebration of his life. I was proud to have got him back home to Ireland for his final resting place. He would now be at peace there forever in the family grave with his mother and father.

I was now back at my house, a few weeks after my Dad's funeral, and I had got to know quite a few people at the local rugby club. They played in the South West leagues, which was a high standard of rugby. I was getting more used to the quieter life, compared to the frantic London life. Daniel was doing well at school, and he had achieved all of the drumming grades up to level eight by the time he was fifteen years old, and all with distinctions. James was still not far away from us, then he moved to live in Croydon for a while and met a lovely girl from there. They moved to Essex for work, and they were very happy.

I had been away on several holidays with my sons over the years, like to the Canary Islands to Bardonecchia in Italy where they once held the Winter Olympics and where we went skiing. It is near the city of Turin. I also went skiing with just Daniel to Austria, but after a couple of days Daniel had a terrible accident. He was on a skiing lesson with one of these ski instructors. You know the sort, who pop up every year at half-term time for some easy money on the slopes. I foolishly trusted him with the safety of my child.

This instructor took them off-piste to this narrow ridge up on the edge of the mountain. They had to ski down one at a time as it was so narrow. This lad was a bit younger than Daniel, and he was a bit apprehensive, so Daniel told him to ski down first. The stupid instructor had already skied down and was waiting around the bend and completely out of view of the people he was supposed to be looking after and teaching. This lad went off and around the bend, then Daniel went off, but as Daniel came around the bend, this young lad had fallen and was laid flat on the snow. Daniel had no choice but to lay down on the snow and slide into the lad's skis, making sure he missed the young lad's body.

The result was that Daniel's arm slid down the sharp edge of the lad's ski, cutting his skin through to the bone. They got Daniel down to a restroom, and I got to see him and go with him to the hospital. They operated on his arm for hours, and eventually he was in a ward full of men. He had been very brave throughout the ordeal. I travelled every day by taxi to and from the hospital, trying to make him as comfortable as possible, with lots of things he could do to occupy himself. He had his whole arm in plaster, bent at the elbow. I nearly hit the instructor when I caught sight of him back at the resort, but I knew it would do no good for Daniel if I deserted him and got locked up.

I did go in to see the main bosses of the ski instructors to complain, hoping they would at least sack him or discipline the idiot, but they all stuck together and told me how hard it was for them to get enough instructors at this time of the year. It was all about self-preservation, and they didn't want an insurance claim. What nice people. After three days Daniel was allowed out of hospital, and I had managed to get us an early flight back home. There really was nothing for us to do, as we could not ski, and that was the only thing we came for. Daniel had his whole arm in plaster for several weeks, and when it was all exposed and the plaster was removed, our doctor commented on how good the Austrian surgeons were. They had done a great job and saved the use of Daniel's arm. Daniel made a full recovery, and the wound healed well, just leaving a nasty scar from his elbow to his wrist.

From 2004 to 2010, I went to Dubai each year with some business friends. They were all company owners like me, and they loved the rugby sevens. We went each year for four days to cover the weekend of the rugby sevens tournament around the first or second of December. Every year we saw Dubai growing, with massive tower blocks and new hotels rising to fifty-something storeys at a time and the tallest building in the world, the Burj Khalifa. Every year it was a few more storeys higher, until we eventually saw it completed.

They were great trips and a lot of fun with likeminded individuals. I remember my first time in Dubai. On my first day staying in this great hotel, I came down to the swimming pool where my friends were relaxing, and as I walked out from the hotel building to the swimming pool, I could hear this very loud chanting or praying coming through the air, from a tall tower nearby. I think it was the Muslim call to prayer.

I said, "Wow! You really know where you are when you hear that," and one of my friends replied, "Yeah, South London." We all laughed. We went horse racing in Dubai, and I really enjoyed the gold souk and the markets and the beach. It was always around 80C when we went, which was very welcome coming from the middle of our winter back home. The food in Dubai is amazing; every single restaurant and hotel has fantastic chefs. It doesn't matter if it's Chinese, Indian, red snapper, lobster, or the finest steaks – it is all incredible. We had a lot of fun just being in Dubai, and the rugby was amazing. You can't put a price on memories. I'd like to thank everyone who came on those trips for their superb company.

In 2010, to celebrate my fiftieth birthday, I went to Dubai on my own. I travelled with first-class flights and I really spoilt myself. On the plane in the first-class cabin, they offer you these Teletubby suits to wear whilst they hang up your suit for the duration of the flight. These are bright green, red, or blue all-in-ones, and they look very silly. I declined to wear one, and I just got myself nice and comfortable in my own pod. I then watched these fully grown businessmen walking about in their Teletubby suits with a flute of champagne in hand or sitting at the bar. It did make me laugh. Don't they realise it is only a seven-hour flight?

I had a whole week on my own in Dubai. Although a bit boring at times, it was nice to relax in the hotel pool with the strong sun above. I visited the now-finished Burj Khalifa, the world's tallest building, with 163 floors. I bought a VIP pass, and I was escorted to my own elevator, which was all in shiny black marble. There was a large man standing inside to operate the elevator. He asked me, "Are you okay with elevators and heights?"

I said, "Yes, I am fine. I was brought up in a London tower block."

He smiled and told me to look up at the ceiling. It had lots of coloured lights darting about. Then the lift stopped, and he said, "Enjoy the view, sir."

I could not believe I had just travelled up to floor number 125 in a few seconds. It is the fastest elevator in the world and completely driven by air – no cables. A remarkable feat of engineering and construction. The viewing platform has since been raised up to floor 148, but I was very happy with floor 125. It was an amazing sight, looking over the whole of Dubai with Abu Dhabi in the distance. I could see the beaches and sea and the Palm development stretching far out into the blue water. After watching this iconic building grow year after year, it was a fantastic feeling to be in this position and on my fiftieth birthday.

I also really enjoyed Cannes and Monte Carlo, in the South of France. I stayed in a very nice hotel on the seafront of Cannes. They had their own quay for their private boat to take you along the coast to see St Tropez. Unfortunately, it only operated in the summer months. They have their own private beach as well. I found out, by going up one floor too many to my room, that they have personal suites on the top floor for very famous Hollywood actors. They even have their name on their room door. I expect it's for the Cannes Film Festival each year. I loved the ambience of Cannes and the laid-back way of life. I sat one day at a small café beside the busy end of the marina, and before I knew it, I had been there for three hours and I had drunk a gallon of coffee. It was just so mesmerising to watch everything going by. The people were so magnetic to watch.

I caught a train to Monte Carlo to watch the tennis tournament. I had never seen live professional tennis before, and it was a real joy to see Andy Murray, Novak Djokovic, and Rafael Nadal play live. Unfortunately, Roger Federer had an injury and didn't enter the tournament. I loved walking through the tunnel at Monte Carlo. I had seen Grand Prix cars racing through it all my life on the TV growing up, and now to be strolling through it was fantastic. The marina was magnificent. I have always loved boats, as did my father. I could not afford to buy one though, and the old quote from Michael Caine springs to mind: "The two happiest people I ever met was a man who had just bought a boat, and a man who had just sold a boat." I had a friend who owned a nice boat, and he told me it was very expensive to look after.

Whilst in Cannes at the marina, I bought a ticket and got on a small boat that went over to a very small island. The island was inhabited and maintained by monks from the monastery on the island. The monks would give tours and talks on the history of the island. They had their own vineyards as well. The biggest attraction on the island was the large old room where the Man in the Iron Mask had been held captive for many years. It was a very big room, with a large old wooden table and chairs. The barred window was up very high. The door was very big and made from immensely thick wood with massive locks on it. Real historic stuff, which was brilliant. I had a whole week in Cannes, which was very relaxing, but I was very lonely. I wished Gabby could be with me on my travels. She has missed out on seeing so much of the world, and I have missed out on sharing my experiences with the woman I love.

Our company was doing okay. After we came through the recession of 2007/2008, we picked up a couple of large contracts. In 2009, we completed several large projects. We went on to build some major schools and hospitals across the country, with some fantastic workmanship. I can honestly say the bricklayers that worked for us were the best I had ever seen in my life. Some of their workmanship was like wallpaper; you could not find faults with it no matter how hard you tried, and our supervisors were first class to sustain such high standards.

In 2013, we were once again voted the No. 1 brickwork contractor in the UK, at the Brick Awards in London. I felt a great sense of achievement for me and my other directors, and everyone who worked with us. It was amazing to win such a prestigious award once again, and six years after previously winning it, we must have been doing something right. I had been working closely with the Association of Brickwork Contractors (ABC) on improving our standing within the construction industry. The very best brickwork contractors were all members of the ABC from across the UK. The brickwork company owners came to our meetings in London from Yorkshire, Midlands, Scotland, and Wales, as well as from all around the home counties and London. Our meetings were aimed at improving the numbers of trained apprentices, health and safety, quality, and collaboration.

Along with others from the ABC and BDA, I spent a lot of time visiting various colleges to discuss with the lecturers the latest advancements in bricklaying. I really enjoyed talking with the apprentices at the colleges, and I think they were boosted to know that I was once in their shoes at college also. One of the main points I would always try to get across to them was, "You must get up every morning and get to work, because if you can't get up in the morning, you are going to have a very difficult life."

I was still going back to London visiting old mates, but I was far more sensible these days. Some of the people we knew had been arrested in a major police operation called Eaglewood. Police had people undercover for twelve months, and they smashed a £100 million cocaine importation gang. Thirty-three people got more than two hundred years in prison. We would probably not see our friends free again, as they could be in prison for the rest of their lives. We were all in our fifties. A close friend of mine's relative had just got twenty years in prison for armed robbery. It would be fair to say the law was winning.

This was the moment when I decided I had to cut my ties with London. It was time for me to grow up and denounce violence and breaking the law. It was the right time to fall back in love with myself once again. They say you cannot love someone else, unless you love yourself. These are true words. I suddenly realised that over all these years, I didn't like myself. I was punishing myself by acting like an idiot. I was risking everything I had worked so hard to achieve. As the Dalai Lama would say, "Short-term pleasure is not as important as long-term happiness."

Chapter Twelve
Finally Growing Up at Sixty Years of Age

I had decided to hang up my gloves and my bad boy past, once and for all. That meant throwing away my address book and phone numbers and starting out fresh. I had recently sent my sons on holiday to ski in Whistler, Canada. They had a great time, and I was very pleased for them both. They deserved the treat as they were both doing well.

James and his girlfriend then moved to New Zealand, as he wanted to help with the rebuilding after the terrible earthquakes of 2016. I was sad to see them living on the other side of the world, but I was proud of his desire to help. They lived in Christchurch, and he helped at a large company assessing the damage and the costs to rebuild. When I spoke with him, he told me they were still getting tremors in the nights. He returned to England after his work was done. He married his girlfriend, and they now have a little boy. They bought their own house and live not far from me.

Daniel did well at school, with ten O levels and three A levels. He is now enjoying his biomedical sciences degree in London. He is living with his fiancée.

In mid-2016, I had to have our dog Jock put down at the vet's. He had partially lost the use of his hindquarters, and he was going blind and deaf. It was time to do the kindest thing an owner can do for his pet and let him go, so he could be free from all the pain and discomfort. I held his face in my hands, and I gently stroked his head as the vet injected his rear leg. He was looking into my eyes with all the love he had, and then he slowly closed them to go to sleep. It was the nicest thing I could do for him. I am not one of those people that say, "Losing a dog is as bad as losing a human." I was very upset, as I loved the dog for being the great pet that he was, but I always knew that one day he would be gone. After all the illness and discomfort he had been through and that I had seen him go through, I had prepared myself for the end. I was very happy with the sixteen years and six months we had with him. My wife and sons all took it well but were naturally also very upset.

One thing I didn't realise was that he had affected my health, as I was allergic to dogs and cats, and I had to use an inhaler twice a day. I didn't mind doing this when we first got the dog, and now that he was gone I stopped using my inhaler, as I thought there was no need. We had the house professionally cleaned, and I was fine for a week or so, then I started having breathing problems. I went to see my doctor, who informed me that as I had been taking an inhaler twice a day for the last sixteen years and six months, my airways had become reliant on it. He explained that your airways can become all knotted up if you stop using an inhaler after that long. I now need to use an inhaler twice a day for the rest of my life. This is not a problem for me, and I wouldn't change anything. I have no regrets of having Jock as our pet. He was a very special dog.

The business was still plodding along, but in January 2017, a large main contractor went bust. We got caught for a lot of money that we will be owed until the day we die. It was such a shame, as the contractor did everything right on site, and they were a pleasure to work for. We had built the stonework, brickwork, and blockwork for them on some fantastic projects around the country. That contractor going bust hurt us immensely, and we struggled to get over it. We continued putting out fires to stay afloat, but I think this unfortunate event changed the entire construction industry. Every main contractor now does not want to be the next one to go bust. From director level down, I have witnessed these changes. Add to that the distinct shortage of experienced site managers, quantity surveyors, and good time-served bricklayers, and you can see why the construction industry is currently in turmoil, in my honest opinion. Brickwork is being replaced more and more by glass and cladding. Where we once built buildings to last hundred years, and whereas I was trained as a bricklayer to have this in mind, we now build buildings with a life span of maybe only twenty years, and we are supposed to achieve this in ridiculously short-programme durations, leading to everything being rushed and, on some sites, to corners being cut.

Gabby and our family have had a very challenging time over the last few years. Gabby's mother died in 2002, and it hit her very hard, prompting an old eating disorder to resurface. Then on New Year's Eve 2016/17, her father was taken into hospital and passed away a month later. Gabby took it hard and went into a decline in her health, and she stopped eating all together, resulting in her being admitted into hospital in 2017. Gabby remained in hospital for six weeks, until they manged to get her weight back up from six stone to nine stone by inserting tubes through her nose to take liquid food to her stomach.

It was great to have her back home, however in 2019 she started to get lots of pains in her right foot. It turned grey in colour and swelled up. After two months of seeing the local doctors, the pain got so bad I took her to the hospital myself on a self-referral, and they immediately took her in. Gabby had two blood clots in her right hip area that were preventing blood from going down her leg to her right foot. Her weight had dropped as well, to only six stone, and they were not sure if she would survive the operation.

My two sons and I were now wandering around the hospital, while the operation was in progress over many hours and well into the night. At times like these, you feel completely useless. At 2:00 a.m., we finally got to see her briefly, in the intensive care unit (ICU), but she was not awake. We went back the following morning, and she was awake but very groggy. The doctor told us they had managed to remove the blood clots, but they would be unable to save the leg, and it would need to be amputated.

The following day Gabby was back in the operating theatre to have her right leg amputated. The operation took three hours, and they amputated the right leg six inches above her right knee. We got to see her briefly back in the ICU, but she was very poorly and wearing an oxygen mask for several days, and the leg was gone. This was all a very stressful time for Daniel, James, and me. It was like our whole world had stopped, and we were struggling to carry on as normal. Eventually Gabby improved and came out of ICU and into a normal room that was far more relaxed.

By the time we got Gabby home, she had been in hospital for ten weeks, with sixteen days of that time in the ICU. To get her home, I had to knock the house about, altering it to be more wheelchair friendly and making her en suite shower into a wet room with a completely flat and tiled floor, enabling her to go all the way into the shower with her wheelchair to a seat.

I was now going to be spending much of my time looking after Gabby and trying to make her life as easy as I could with her new disability. This led to me having to accept that the end was near for the brickwork company. I couldn't work with the correct intensity required to run a large business properly. My fellow directors understood the position, and we agreed now was the right time to finish. We are now in the process of selling the company office building and closing the company down. I cannot afford to fully retire, and I will have to get a job soon; that will be the next hurdle in my life.

My mother moved into a nursing home in Essex in 2013, and I visited her every other Saturday for five years until she passed away in 2018. Just nine days before her ninety-seventh birthday. What a remarkable woman, to have lived the life she had and to survive that long. We had a small family funeral for her that my sister Freda organised, complete with a Scottish piper in front of the hearse. A few of my relatives came down from Scotland – that was much appreciated – and both my father and mother would have loved that. As was her wish, my mother is now buried close to my nephew in the same graveyard in Hertfordshire. I thought after the funeral, *I am coming up to fifty-eight years old, and I am now an orphan.*

If there is one thing we should discuss more with our children, it's how their life may change after us parents have passed away. We cannot get away from the fact we are all going to die one day. My sister Molly told me years ago how when she was with my father over in Ireland in 1966, at his father's deathbed, she was heavily pregnant with her first child, and she held her granddad's hand in his last few minutes, before he passed away.

Molly said to him, "I feel so guilty sitting here with a new baby in my belly and you passing away."

He raised his head and said slowly, "That's exactly how it should be – one passes and another comes in. That's how it should be."

Although both my parents have now passed away, I have only a couple of regrets: me getting put into prison, and how I should have been nicer to my mother when I was in my teens. There is a funny thing that happened to me a month after my father died. I broke out in a rash, and I began to suffer with dry skin on my legs. Then I started to have all sorts of fears.

I've always been a bit claustrophobic, as I've been stuck in a lift no less than three times in my life. I bet not many people can say that. The claustrophobia became more challenging and started happening every day, and I'm talking about whilst sitting in a traffic jam, or in a pub that starts to fill up. Going to a stadium event or concert, I found I couldn't sit in the middle of a row. I had to be on the aisle seat. Flying, I had to have an aisle seat, whereas I used to love sitting by the window. In all these cases my breathing would become difficult, and my heart rate would accelerate. The doctor said it could be stress, anxiety, or perhaps delayed shock and mourning for my father. One thing I knew for sure was that, before my father died, I was invincible and fearless, and now that he was gone, I felt vulnerable, and I had fears that had crept up on me.

In the next few years, I would work hard mentally to overcome these fears. They are still there, but I have a better understanding of them now, and I can accept them and work with my brain to control them to a certain extent. I found the audiobook *The Chimp Paradox* by Steve Peters a great help, and I would advise anyone to listen to it fully over a short period of time. I listened to it every day for a month whilst driving. It calmed me down, and it gave me a complete and much better understanding of what was going on in my head.

I had one very special night when I did not worry about anything, and that was my fifty-seventh birthday in 2017. My two sons and a good friend of mine who was football mad came with me to Wembley to see Tottenham Hotspur FC v. Real Madrid in a Champions League football match. We were in nice hospitality, and we met a few ex-players. My friend was chuffed to meet *The Swansea Express* Cliff Jones, who he had seen play many years ago. Tottenham's new £500 million stadium was still under construction, so they were playing all their matches at the new Wembley Stadium. We had a fantastic night that I was so pleased and proud to share with my two sons. Tottenham won 3–1 as well. Real Madrid's first-ever visit to Wembley ended in a loss to the mighty Spurs.

Life has been moving along steadily. I never drink alcohol at home. I need to be in a social environment to drink alcohol. It's all about the company and the surroundings for me. I played skittles for a few years with an excellent mid-table team in our local club. My fellow players were all good fun to be around, and we had a lot of fun. Our opponents were also lots of fun, and it was always an entertaining night at our skittle matches.

After going through all the trauma and the problems with Gabby, I stopped playing skittles. I couldn't explain why, it was just that it wasn't something I could do happily, after what I had been through. It was going to take some time for me to be truly happy once again. I don't go out during the week anymore. I only go out on Friday and Saturday nights now, and that suits me just fine. I really look forward to a night out after the whole week indoors. I sit with fantastic mates who are from nearby places. It's very different than London – not better or worse, just different. The pubs are far quieter than London, and although you still have your tough and very hard men, there are naturally less of them than in the overpopulated city of London. We sit around a table telling funny stories and jokes, mostly with just us men, but on the odd occasion we allow women to join us, but only as platonic friends. The club is well organised and has a great couple running it. There is live music every week, a great bar with a good jukebox, two full-size snooker tables in a separate snooker room upstairs, a pool table, and a dart board, and they have weekly raffles with lots of prizes for anyone to win, which is run by volunteers who are great people. The whole club is full of decent people of all ages, and it's a nice place to be on a weekend night.

When I look back on my life, I feel there were times when I wasn't a very nice person. I am not going to blame anyone or any circumstances for that. It was all down to me and me alone. Yes, I agree that every one of us could've had been brought up in better circumstances that may have shaped our lives differently, but we just got on with it and lived with whatever hand we were dealt.

I like to think I am now a much nicer and better person after all the experiences I have been through. I am now quite content with my life, and I feel great joy when feeding the birds and the squirrels who visit my garden every day. I still have the beast within, though, and there are sometimes when I feel like I am a powder keg or an unexploded bomb just waiting to go off. I must be careful to avoid tricky confrontations with people, especially people who know nothing about me. I have many memories, some good and some bad, and at times I miss those mad times with the bizarre goings-on, and the danger. I can accept the quiet life these days, and over the years I've learnt that my life needs meaning and purpose to be fulfilling. I have had to change my outlook on life many times.

Will we ever be truly happy? I am not sure of the answer to that, and in my own personal case, I can only say I'm as happy as I can be, allowing for my current position and circumstances. I believe there is no holy grail for the enchanted and perfect life. Life is as happy as you expect it to be. We all have a different barometer of life, with different expectations. We all accept different levels of what gives us fulfilment and happiness. We must all train our brain and thoughts towards happiness. This is called inner discipline, and if achieved, it can bring a much happier and better life for you.

I read a book called *The Art of Happiness*, written by the Dalai Lama and Howard C. Cutler. In a section called 'Basic Spiritual Values', they write, "The art of happiness has many components. As we've seen, it begins with developing an understanding of the truest sources of happiness and setting out priorities in life based on the cultivation of those sources. It involves an inner discipline, a gradual process of rooting out destructive mental states, and replacing them with positive, constructive states of mind, such as kindness, tolerance, and forgiveness."

Those are indeed wise words. I have worked very hard over the past few years to bring myself to this tranquil position I am now enjoying. I no longer feel ashamed of my past. I accept it, as I was always a person who was on an adventure to discover the good and the bad in life.

I apologise to anyone who is not mentioned in this book, and who feels they should have been. I can only say if I had included everything in it, it would take someone fifty-nine years to read it. I must also apologise to anyone I hit or who I caused pain. I realise now that was the wrong action to take at the time, but I knew no different. I was a broken human.

I am very grateful to my children and Gabby for sticking with me and eventually seeing the real me. I thank all my siblings and relatives, who have all done their best in life, and they have been there if I ever needed any of them. I can categorically say ALL my children, Gabby, and my brothers, sisters, and relatives are completely different from me. They are all law-abiding citizens who have lived their lives completely differently to mine. We are like chalk and cheese, and I am the black sheep of the family. I apologise to all of them, especially if any of them feel ashamed or embarrassed by this book and its contents. That was never my intention. Sorry.

My biggest thank-you is to both my parents, for bringing me up to the best of their knowledge. There are no university degrees for parenthood. Every new parent must bring up their child in the way they think is the best for that child and themselves in their circumstances. We can all have opinions, and we can all think we know best, but we do not always.

I've had the nickname Roger the boxer since after I left school. People in the pubs I previously mentioned in this book would say to someone, "Do you know Roger?" and they would reply, "Roger who?" and then they would say, "You know, Roger the boxer," and they would reply, "Oh yeah, everyone knows Roger the boxer."

To the readers: I hope you have enjoyed reading this book and that it has made you realise the importance of treasuring your life, and to enjoy it every day without fears. Time stands still for no one. Like an old friend of mine often says, "You only get one lap of the track." There is nothing better than relaxing and reading an interesting book, and I hope this has been an interesting read for you.

In conclusion, I am just passing through. I am now no longer a fighter, and I am at peace with myself and the world. Thank you, from plain old Roger.

CPSIA information can be obtained
at www.ICGtesting.com
Printed in the USA
LVHW082237310122
709794LV00026B/298